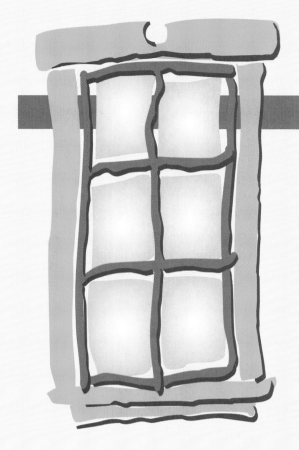

THE INTERNET

A TUTORIAL

TO ACCOMPANY

PETER NORTON'S

INTRODUCTION

TO COMPUTERS

JOHN ROSS

GLENCOE

MCGRAW-HILL

NEW YORK, NEW YORK • COLUMBUS, OHIO • MISSION HILLS, CALIFORNIA • PEORIA, ILLINOIS

The Internet
A Tutorial to Accompany
Peter Norton's Introduction to Computers

Send all inquiries to:
Glencoe/McGraw-Hill
936 Eastwind Drive
Westerville, OH 43081

ISBN 0-02-802963-1

Concept, Development, and Production: Jennings & Keefe Media Development, Corte Madera, California
   Editorial Management: Karen Lamoreux
   Developmental Editing: Pete Alcorn
   Technical Editing: Jane Hurford
   Design: Randall Goodall
   Production Management: Rad Proctor
   Copyediting: Mary Ellen Korman
   Electronic Composition: Rad Proctor
   Indexing: Anne Leach

1 2 3 4 5 6 7 8 9 POH 01 00 99 98 97 96

CONTENTS

LESSON 3
INTERNET NEWS

LESSON 4
TELNET AND FTP: OPERATING
DISTANT COMPUTERS
AND OBTAINING FILES

This *Internet Tutorial* is one of the instructional tools that complement *Peter Norton's Introduction to Computers*. Glencoe and Peter Norton have teamed up to provide a new approach to computer education, one not reflected in traditional computer textbooks. The text and its ancillary materials are grounded in the philosophy that knowledgeable, empowered end users will provide the gains in productivity that both businesses and individuals need in the 1990s and beyond. Mere button pushing is not enough; in order to handle increasingly complex computer tasks, both in the workplace and at home, computer users must understand the concepts behind their computer hardware and software.

STRUCTURE AND FORMAT OF THE INTERNET TUTORIAL

This book exposes you to a wide range of Internet functions and tools. You will learn that the Internet offers several ways to connect your computer to other computers, which may be located almost anywhere in the world. Because the Internet is such a rich collection of resources, practicing new functions and techniques is an important part of your work. To help you practice, each lesson includes the following:

- *Explanations of important concepts.* Each section in every lesson begins with an explanation of the concept or program being covered in that lesson. The explanations help you understand "the big picture" as you learn each new facet of the program.

- *New terms in boldface.* An important part of learning about computers is learning the terminology. Each new term in the text is set in **boldface** and defined the first time that it is used. As you encounter these words, read their definitions carefully. If you encounter the same word later and have forgotten its meaning, you can look it up in the Glossary at the back of the book.

- *Step-by-step instructions.* Because most students learn best by doing, each explanation is followed by a concise set of steps, which you complete at the computer. As you perform the steps, you will be sending and receiving messages and moving around the Internet to view documents and other files located on computers around the world.

- *Many illustrations.* As you work through the tutorial, you will find many figures that help you stay on track. The figures are used to point out features on the screen and illustrate what your screen should look like after important steps are completed.

■ *Review exercises.* At the end of each lesson, you will find three types of objective questions: a matching exercise, completion exercise, and short-answer questions. Completing these exercises will help you make sure that you have learned all the concepts and skills that have been covered in the lesson.

■ *Application projects.* The last element in each lesson is a set of Application Projects that can give you extra hands-on practice using your problem-solving skills and the techniques you have learned in the lesson to find and download actual Internet resources.

After you complete this book, you will have the skills necessary to send and receive electronic mail through the Internet, read and participate in Internet news groups, and use a variety of methods to connect your PC to other systems on the Internet.

LOADING THE INTERNET TOOLS

Unlike other tutorials in this series that describe specific application programs, the *Internet Tutorial* includes typical tools that demonstrate the most common ways to use the Internet. Mastering these tools will help the student understand the general concepts needed to navigate the Internet.

The programs described in this tutorial are available free from online sources:

Eudora	electronic mail
Trumpet News	news reader
Trumpet Telnet	VT-100 terminal emulator
QWS 3270	IBM 3270 terminal emulator
WS-FTP	file transfer
WS Gopher	Gopher client
WS Ping	Ping utility
Finger	Finger utility
Netscape Navigator	World Wide Web browser
Trumpet Winsock	TCP/IP Windows Socket interface and dialer

These programs have probably been installed on the hard drive of each computer in the lab at your school, and you will be instructed on how to use them. If the programs have not been installed on the computer you are using, your instructor or lab assistant will install them for you or give you copies of the programs and tell you how to install them.

All of these programs, except Trumpet Winsock and Trumpet News, are freeware (the software developers have made them available at no charge). The Trumpet programs are shareware, which means if you choose to use the program on computers outside of your classroom or computer lab, you are expected to send the developer a registration fee.

This tutorial is not intended to be a complete guide to all of the features and functions of the programs used in the demonstrations. For more detailed information about these programs, consult the user manuals that are supplied with the software.

SETTING UP THE COMPUTER LAB: WHAT MUST BE DONE BEFORE YOU USE THIS TUTORIAL

The programs described in this tutorial require a connection to the Internet through a local area network and an interface program called a Winsock (Windows Socket) stack.

The PCs in the computer lab at your school probably have this type of connection. It is also possible to use these programs with a telephone line and modem connection to a SLIP or PPP account. Once they have been installed, the Internet application programs will automatically find the Winsock stack and establish your connection to the Internet.

ABOUT PETER NORTON

Peter Norton is a pioneering software developer and author. Norton's Desktop for Windows, Utilities, Backup, AntiVirus, and other utility programs are installed on countless PCs worldwide. His *Inside the IBM PC* and *DOS Guide* have helped millions of people understand computers from the inside out.

Glencoe has teamed up with this trusted name in computers to help you better understand the role computers play in your life. You may use this resource as a textbook now and a reference book later as you begin your productive use of computers in your chosen profession.

REVIEWERS

Many thanks are due to Mark Hall, Spokane Community College; David Letcher, Trenton State College; and Theresa TenEyck, Boise State University; who reviewed the manuscript and gave advice on how to improve the book.

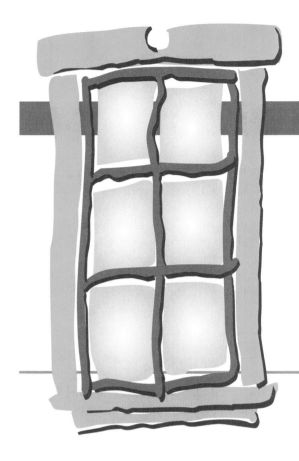

LESSON 1

INTRODUCTION TO

THE INTERNET

OBJECTIVES

After completing this lesson, you will be able to do the following:

- *Know something about the history of the Internet.*
- *Understand how the Internet is organized.*
- *Recognize and use Internet addresses.*
- *Connect your computer to the Internet.*
- *Know about different kinds of Internet services.*

f you believe all the publicity about the Internet, you might think it's a giant water pipe plugged into the back of your computer, spewing gallons and gallons of information through your screen. That's not quite correct. The Internet, technically speaking, is a "network of networks" that connects together millions of computers all over the world. It allows users to share messages, programs, and other information. It's not so much a water pipe as a candy store where you can choose the goodies you want to sample.

ABOUT THE INTERNET AND ITS HISTORY

Internet The Internet is the world-wide interconnected network of computers that can exchange messages, commands, and data.

The **Internet** is described as a network of networks, but that's not very helpful unless you know what a network is. You're familiar with many kinds of networks. The world-wide telephone system that connects the phone in your kitchen to millions of others around the world is a network. The streets and highways that let you start from your own driveway and travel to Yellowstone National Park make up another network. The characteristic that these networks have in common is that they use some kind of standard design to connect things to one another.

Some networks are more technically complicated and less forgiving than others. For example, you can use the same road system to drive a car, pedal a bicycle, or walk. But unless you have a telephone that produces exactly the right kind of signals, you won't be able to place calls through the telephone network at all.

When you connect two or more computers together and exchange data among them, you have created another kind of network. People using computers connected through a network can generally send and receive messages to other users; run programs and read files from any computer on the network; and use printers, storage devices such as disk or tape drives, and other resources located anywhere on the network.

A business might create a network so employees in one department can share resources and information. Eventually, somebody in the purchasing department will need something from Engineering, and they'll connect the Engineering network to the Purchasing network to create a pair of *interconnected networks*, or an *internet* (but not *The* Internet). Over time, more local networks will get connected, and as each new network joins, all the others will have access to the computers on that network, even if there's no direct connection between the source and the destination.

That's roughly how the Internet got started. In the late 1960s, when a small computer was the size of four or five refrigerators, the U.S. Department of Defense created an experimental program called ARPANET that connected computers at several universities and government contractors into a network that extended across the United States. It allowed users to remotely operate computers that might be located thousands of miles away, and made it possible for researchers and engineers in different cities to work together on the same project at the same time. And a few months after the system was created in 1969, a college student in California was playing chess on a computer in Massachusetts.

Over time, more and more computers joined this giant interconnected network; it crossed the Atlantic Ocean to England and Norway in 1973. By the early 1990s, there were several million computers around the world connected to the Internet.

EVERYTHING IS CONNECTED TO EVERYTHING ELSE

The Internet can connect your computer to millions of other computers, all over the world (and in outer space—there have been live Internet connections to the Space Shuttle in orbit). Therefore, if you know how to set up a connection, you can exchange messages, programs, and data files with any other computer on the Internet. In many cases, the resources located on any other computer on the Internet are as easy to use as the ones located on your own computer's hard drive.

Many companies, educational institutions, government agencies, and individual people have placed documents, pictures, programs, and other resources on computers that are connected to the Internet. So it's also a gigantic storehouse of easily available material of all kinds. If you know where to look, you can find pictures of famous paintings from the Louvre Museum in Paris or photos from the Hubble Space Telescope; participate in discussions about every imaginable topic with people around the world; download thousands of free or inexpensive programs for your PC; and find out about earthquakes, volcanic eruptions, and other natural disasters almost as soon as they happen.

The Internet is like the line from that old song about a trumpet: "The music goes round and round and it comes out here." In most cases, it's probably easier to think about it that way than to worry about its internal operation. You send your message in, and it comes out someplace else. Somebody else puts the data in, and it "comes out here," in your computer. In between, there's a lot of routing and switching, but that's all more or less automatic.

To put it another way, just as you need to know how and where to put the address on an envelope you drop in a letter box—but don't care if it goes by truck, train, or pack mule—you can use the Internet without any detailed knowledge of networking theory.

When people draw diagrams showing how networks connect to the Internet (like the one in Figure 1-1), they usually show the Internet itself as a big cloud. It's too dark inside that cloud to see what's happening, and besides, your data usually zips right through in a fraction of a second.

protocol A set of signals and commands that computers use to communicate with one another.

All the computers on the Internet must use the same set of signals and commands in order to understand each other. Computer experts call this kind of language a **protocol**. The Internet uses a set of protocols called **TCP/IP**, which stands for Transmission Control Protocol/Internet Protocol.

TCP/IP Transmission Control Protocol/Internet Protocol. The base protocols that are the rules for data format and transmission governing communication over the Internet.

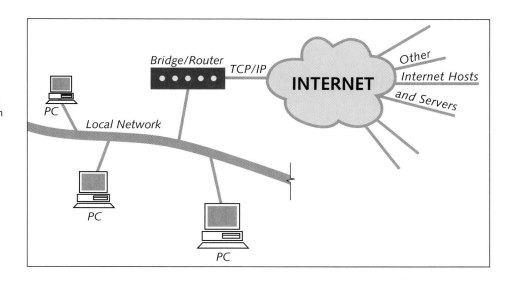

FIGURE 1-1

A typical Internet connection

USING INTERNET ADDRESSES

address The identity of a location on the Internet.

Every computer connected to the Internet, and every person with an account on one of those computers, has a unique **address**, or location on the Internet. In order to communicate with a computer on a distant system, you must use that system's address to identify it. When you want to send somebody a message, you must use that person's Internet address in the heading of your message.

If you think about it, this is not much different from the way you use other networks, like the telephone and mail systems. When you mail a letter to your niece, you can't just write "Susie" on the envelope; you must include a full name, street address, and city. When you make a telephone call, you have to use the number of the telephone line assigned to the person you want to reach. On the Internet, the equivalent of a phone number or postal address usually looks something like this: *fredu@qcc.edu*.

The Internet uses two different systems to define addresses: one system uses numbers, and the other uses words. Every location on the Internet has a four-part numeric address, and most also have a word address. The computers on the Internet could operate quite well with numeric addresses only, but human beings are generally more comfortable with words. Since words are easier to remember than numbers, the Internet uses a database called the **Domain Name Server** that automatically converts names to numbers.

Domain Name Server A database that converts names to numbers, specifically Domain Name System addresses to numeric IP addresses.

IP Address Internet Protocol Address. An Internet address in numeric format.

The number address is called an Internet Protocol address, usually abbreviated to **IP Address**. An IP address contains routing information that the Internet needs to find a specific computer. Every IP address has four parts, with periods separating them. Each part is a number between 0 and 255. For example, an IP address might look like this: 183.206.64.1.

Domain Name System
The Internet address format identifies locations on the Internet by domains such as .edu, .org, and .fr.

domain Part of an address that identifies the type of organization, such as .edu for education; or the part that identifies the geographical location of the addressee, such as .fr for France.

The other method the Internet uses to identify computers is called the **Domain Name System** or DNS. A DNS address has two parts called **domains**. In North America, most (but not all) addresses include a three-letter domain name that shows the type of organization that uses this address. For example, schools, colleges, and other educational institutions use addresses that end with .edu, such as unc.edu for the University of North Carolina. Businesses have addresses with .com (for commercial) as the last part, so Microsoft's DNS address is microsoft.com.

Here are the most commonly used major domain names:

.edu	Colleges, universities and other educational institutions
.com	Commercial businesses
.gov	Government agencies
.mil	Military
.net	Network support centers
.org	Miscellaneous organizations

Major domains are for identification purposes only; a .com or .edu address doesn't limit your access to other users on the Internet. You can easily send messages to systems with government or military domain names.

Most Internet addresses outside North America use two-letter geographical domain names. For example, a DNS address that ends in .fr is in France, and one that ends in .nz is in New Zealand. A few American addresses also use this system.

sub-domain A portion of a DNS address that identifies a smaller group within a larger domain name, such as history.iowa.edu. where history is a sub-domain of the University of Iowa.

Some domain names have many thousands of users, but other organizations prefer to split themselves into smaller groups, called **sub-domains**. So a company with branches in different cities could use a different sub-domain for each branch: you might have denver.megacorp.com and boston.megacorp.com. Or a college could use a sub-domain for each department, such as history.qcc.edu. A sub-domain can also be divided into sub-domains. Therefore, you might see something like ancient.history.qcc.edu.

The general rule for DNS addresses is that they start with the smallest division and each additional word describes a larger group than the one to its left. All DNS addresses end with either a major domain or a geographical domain.

USER NAMES

e-mail address The name and location of an Internet (or other electronic communication service) user, such as *fredu@qcc.edu.*

user name The name that a computer uses to identify a particular user. Used to send and receive mail. In the e-mail address *fredu@qcc.edu,* fredu is the user name.

There's one more element to the system: individual users. Most Internet DNS addresses are either mainframe computers or local networks that are used by more than one person. When you send a message, you must identify the person that you want to receive it by using that person's specific **e-mail address**. An e-mail address is the place where people receive messages through the Internet or other communication services.

When you obtain an account on a computer connected to the Internet, the system administrator assigns you a **user name** that you must use when you **log in**, or start using that computer. That's also the name that other people will use to send you messages. Your personal Internet address is your login name, followed by the "at" symbol (@), and the DNS address of the

log in The process of entering a user's name and password into a computer, in order to start using the computer.

computer where you have the account. So e-mail addresses look like this: *fredu@history.qcc.edu*.

When it's spoken, the @ symbol is read as "at" and the period as "dot." Therefore, you would read *fredu@history.qcc.edu* as "Fred U at history dot Q C C dot E D U." The choice of words or individual letters depends on how easy it might be to pronounce a group of letters. "Dot com" or "dot net" are almost always spoken as words, but "dot ed-yew" (.edu—edu for education) is usually spelled out. Since the Internet is completely unforgiving about typing errors in addresses, it's a good idea when you're telling someone your address to spell out any name that might be easily confused.

CONNECTING YOUR COMPUTER TO THE INTERNET

You're taking this class because you want to learn about the Internet and how to use it. In the remaining lessons in this book, you will learn how to exchange mail, transfer files, operate distant computers across the Internet, and about methods for locating resources online. But before you can do any of these things, you must connect your own computer to the Internet. The computers in your classroom are already connected, but if you want to use the Internet from home, or if your office isn't already online, you'll need to know something about setting up an Internet connection. You can find a directory of Internet service providers online at *http://thelist.com/*. You will learn how to download and read HTTP files in Chapter 6.

Remember the description of the Internet as a big cloud? It might be slightly more useful to think of it as a big cloud with several million wires hanging out of it, each one plugged into a computer. In order to use the Internet yourself, you must first find a way to plug one of those wires into your own PC.

In order to send and receive messages and data through the Internet, a computer must either recognize TCP/IP or go through a second computer that converts to and from some other protocol. There are several ways to attach your computer to the Internet:

SLIP Serial Line Interface Protocol. A data format used to connect a PC to the Internet, using the PC's serial port.

PPP Point-to-Point Protocol. A data format used to connect a PC to the Internet.

remote terminal A terminal or other input and output device connected to a computer through the Internet or some other network.

shell account An account on a host computer that uses the host's command line interface to connect a PC as a remote terminal. A shell account is not a direct connection to the Internet.

- Through a Local Area Network (LAN), such as an office network or a college computer lab that is already connected.

- Through a serial communications port to a network, using either Serial Line Interface Protocol (**SLIP**) or Point-to-Point Protocol (**PPP**).

When you use either of these methods, your computer is connected directly to the Internet, which will run a set of TCP/IP application programs on your PC.

- As a **remote terminal** on a host computer connected to the Internet. A remote terminal sends commands and data with a host computer through a network such as the Internet. This kind of connection is called a **shell account** because it uses a set of commands on the host computer called a shell. When you connect as a remote terminal, the host performs the conversion to TCP/IP. The Internet application programs actually run on the host computer rather than on your PC. You can use a modem and a communications program, such as Procom or CrossTalk, to connect to a host through a telephone line.

- Through a gateway from an online information service such as CompuServe, America Online, or Microsoft Network. The online services all offer Internet access, but they may not be as flexible as a direct connection. Each service uses a different set of Internet commands as part of its graphical user interface.

UUCP Unix to Unix CoPy. A store-and-forward system for exchange of e-mail and news to and from computers that are not directly connected to the Internet.

- Through a store-and-forward system called **UUCP** (Unix to Unix CoPy) that connects through dial-out telephone links on a regular schedule, and exchanges messages that have arrived since the last connection. UUCP is limited to mail and news, and it's not as fast as a live connection, but it can cost less than other kinds of Internet service.

The TCP/IP protocols include a set of standard commands and programs that are the same on many different kinds of computers. The lessons in this book use graphical Internet programs that run on a PC with Microsoft Windows. As you work with them, you will also learn about the general principles that the Internet uses to move different kinds of commands, files, and messages between computers. Once you understand how to use these Internet tools, it doesn't matter if you're working with a Desktop PC or a terminal on a huge supercomputer. You might have to type individual commands instead of using the drag and drop features of a Windows program, but the result will be the same.

THE INTERNET AND WINDOWS: THE WINSOCK STANDARD

Earlier in this chapter, you learned that the Internet uses a set of protocols called TCP/IP. When you connect a PC directly to the Internet, through either a LAN or a serial connection, you must use a TCP/IP program.

When you connect your PC directly to the Internet, you have to do two things at the same time: you must maintain the connection between your computer and the rest of the Internet, and you must run an application program, such as file transfer or remote control of another computer. This would not be a problem if every PC used the same kind of connection to the Internet, but since they don't, you need a different **driver** for each type of hookup. A driver is a piece of software that contains specific connection information. It would be a huge nuisance for the people who create Internet application software if they needed a different version of each application program for every possible type of network connection, so they have agreed to use a standard interface called Windows Sockets, or **Winsock**.

Figure 1-2 shows how the Winsock standard works. Any Winsock-compatible application can communicate with any network interface that uses the Winsock specifications. The interface between the application programs and the network drivers is called a **Winsock stack**.

All Winsock stacks look the same to an application program that is Winsock compatible. Therefore, you can use any Winsock-compatible application program with any Winsock stack program; you're not limited to programs from a single software developer.

driver A set of instructions in software which convert commands from an application program to the format required by a specific communications device.

Winsock The Windows Sockets standard that defines the interface between Internet application programs and network connection drivers.

Winsock stack An interface program that converts signals between Winsock-compliant Internet application programs and network drivers.

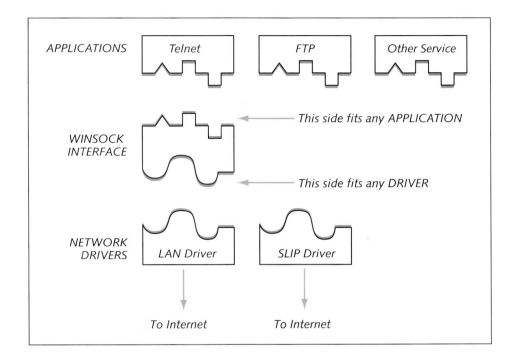

FIGURE 1-2

How a Winsock stack
provides an interface
between applications
and networks

This approach has several advantages. If you find a new application with lots of neat new features, it's no problem to replace the one you've been using because it will work with your existing network connection. And if you change connection methods from, say, a dial-in modem link to a LAN, you don't have to scrap the applications you've already installed.

Since all Winsock stacks present the same appearance to application programs, they all have the same name—WINSOCK.DLL. There's a Winsock stack included in the Windows 95 package, and you can also find one in Internet access software packages from other software publishers. The application programs described in this book are all Winsock compatible.

INTERNET SERVICES

client A computer that requests information or services from another computer through a network.

server A computer that supplies data or services to a client.

As you learn about various Internet services, you will see some computers or programs described as **clients,** and others as **servers.** A client is a computer (or a program running on a computer) that requests information or services through a network. A server is the computer or program that supplies information to a client. In general, the Internet programs that you use on your PC are clients that obtain data from servers located elsewhere on the Internet.

E-MAIL

The single most common activity on the Internet is the exchange of messages, also known as electronic mail, or e-mail. In most cases, the Internet can deliver an e-mail message to its destination in less than an hour; in many cases, the recipient can be reading your message just a minute or two after you send it. Figure 1-3 shows an e-mail message displayed in

Eudora, a mail manager program where you can create outbound messages and read inbound mail, which you will do in Lesson 2.

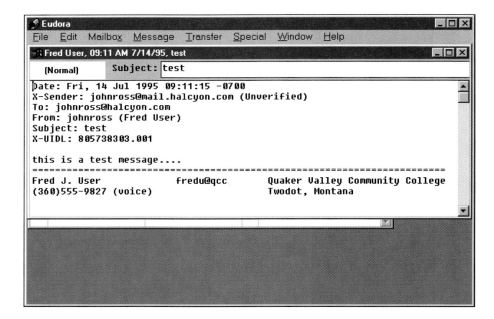

FIGURE 1-3
An e-mail message received in Eudora

NEWS

In addition to sending one-to-one messages through the Internet, it's also possible to send one-to-many messages that are distributed to readers around the world. There are online public discussions, called news groups, devoted to thousands of different topics ranging from particle physics and Norwegian politics to Japanese monster movies and cookie recipes. For example, Figure 1-4 shows Trumpet News, a news reader program that organizes and displays news articles from many different news groups.

REMOTE LOGIN

telnet The Internet service protocol that connects one computer to a second computer as a remote terminal.

If you have an account on a computer connected to the Internet, you can connect your Desktop PC to that machine through the Internet and use the PC as a remote terminal. There are also many systems, such as the ones that contain library catalogs, that allow remote access to anybody who wants to connect. The standard Internet command for remote access to another system is **telnet**. Telnet programs connect your PC to another computer through the Internet. Figure 1-5 shows a remote connection using telnet.

FILE TRANSFER

FTP File Transfer Protocol. The Internet service that moves files between computers.

You're familiar with the file structure that your PC uses to organize and store programs and data; just about every computer on the Internet uses a similar system. The Internet's **File Transfer Protocol** (FTP) is a tool for

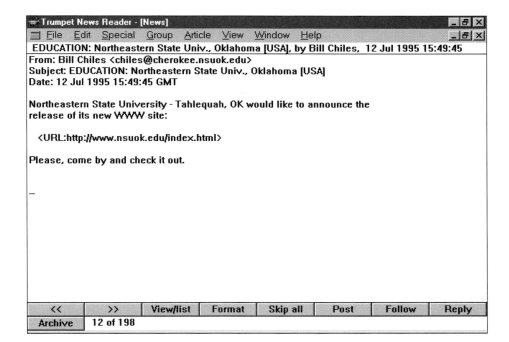

FIGURE 1-4

*A Usenet News article
displayed in Trumpet News*

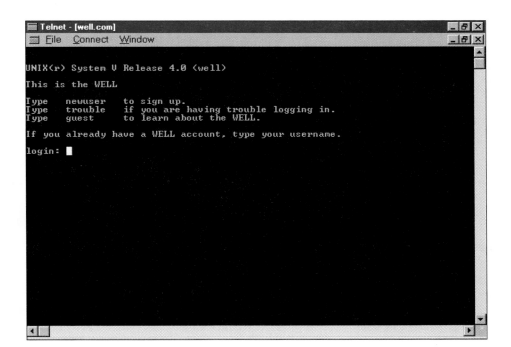

FIGURE 1-5

*A telnet connection
to a conference service*

moving files from one computer to another. There are collections of files on many computers around the world that are available to anybody who wants a copy, including software for your PC (and for many other types of computers), and files that contain text, pictures, and sound recordings. Figure 1-6 shows a Windows utility for FTP file transfer.

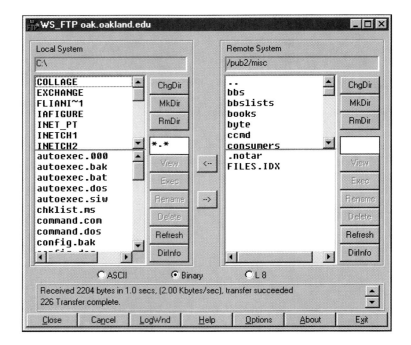

FIGURE 1-6

An FTP file transfer using WS-FTP

GOPHER

The Internet Gopher is a system of menus that organizes Internet resources into logical groups. When you select an item from a Gopher menu, you immediately jump to that item, which might be another menu, or a document, picture, audio file, or even a telnet remote login to a distant computer.

Figure 1-7 shows WS Gopher, a Windows-based Gopher client that gives you point-and-click access to the Internet through Gopher menus.

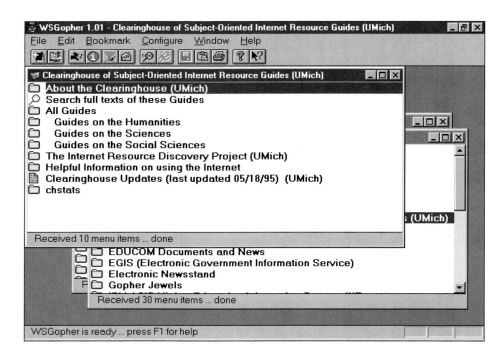

FIGURE 1-7

Gopher menus displayed in the WS Gopher client

THE WORLD WIDE WEB

The World Wide Web pulls together many other Internet tools and services and ties them up in an attractive graphic package. A "web page" can include both text and pictures, along with jumps to other files that can be located anywhere on the Internet. Even more than other services, the World Wide Web can make Internet resources anywhere in the world as easy to use as those on your own computer.

Figure 1-8 shows a screen from Netscape Navigator, a World Wide Web browser that you will use in Lesson 6.

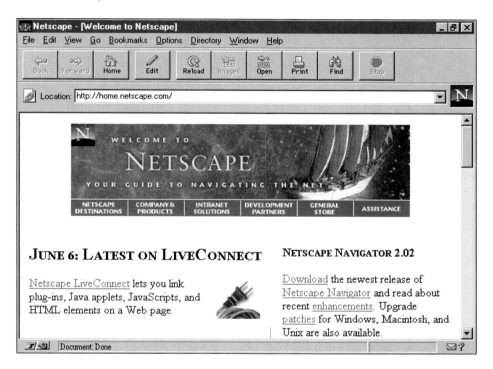

FIGURE 1-8

A World Wide Web page in Netscape Navigator

To summarize, the Internet is a giant network of several million computers that all use TCP/IP protocols to exchange messages, programs, and data. The Winsock standard is a program interface that connects PCs running Microsoft Windows to the Internet. In the remaining lessons of this book, you will learn how to use a collection of Winsock-compatible application programs to send and receive messages through the Internet, connect your computer to other computers through the Internet, run programs on the distant system, transfer files back to your PC from other computers around the world, and use several Internet navigation tools, including the Internet Gopher and a World Wide Web browser.

- In Lesson 2, you will learn about electronic mail, and how to use Eudora, a widely-used mail handling application program.

- Lesson 3 describes Internet News, the Trumpet News news reader program.

- Lesson 4 tells you about the two most common services for connecting your PC directly to another computer through the Internet. These services are telnet, which allows you to remotely log into a distant system, and FTP, the File Transfer Protocol used for moving files between computers.

■ Lesson 5 describes Gopher, the structured system that organizes Internet resources into menus. In this lesson, you will learn how to use WS Gopher, a graphical Gopher client program.

■ Lesson 6 explains the World Wide Web, which provides a single graphical tool for importing many different kinds of Internet resources. It also describes Netscape Navigator, a World Wide Web browser program.

■ Lesson 7 contains information about several Internet utilities: Ping, Finger, and Archie. Ping tests connections across the Internet by sending a request for an echo; Finger obtains information about users of distant systems; and Archie is a search tool for locating files in FTP archives.

LESSON SUMMARY AND EXERCISES

After completing this lesson, you should know how to do the following:

ABOUT THE INTERNET AND ITS HISTORY

- The Internet grew and developed from a network originally established by the U.S. Department of Defense to connect computers and users in many locations.

EVERYTHING IS CONNECTED TO EVERYTHING ELSE

- Any computer connected to the Internet can share messages, data files, and programs with any other computer on the Internet.

- All computers on the Internet use the same set of signals and commands, called TCP/IP.

USING INTERNET ADDRESSES

- There are two kinds of Internet addresses: four-part numbers (IP addresses), and Domain Name System (DNS) addresses.

CONNECTING YOUR COMPUTER TO THE INTERNET

- Your computer may be connected to the Internet through a LAN (Local Area Network), through a serial line connection using SLIP or PPP protocols, through a gateway from an online information service, or as a remote terminal on another computer.

THE INTERNET AND WINDOWS: THE WINSOCK STANDARD

- Internet application programs for Windows use the Winsock specification as the interface between application programs and Internet connections.

INTERNET SERVICES

- E-mail is the exchange of messages and files through the Internet, or commercial electronic mail services that may also provide Internet access.

- News is the system that distributes public messages on many subjects.

- Telnet is the Internet tool that connects your computer to a distant computer as a remote terminal.

- FTP moves data files and programs between computers.

- Gopher organizes Internet resources into hierarchical menus.

- The World Wide Web uses links to allow a user to jump between documents and other Internet resources and services.

NEW TERMS TO REMEMBER

After completing this lesson, you should know the meaning of these terms:

address	protocol
client	remote terminal
domain	server
Domain Name Server	shell account
Domain Name System	SLIP
driver	sub-domain
e-mail address	TCP/IP
File Transfer Protocol (FTP)	telnet
Internet	user name
log in	UUCP
IP Address	Winsock
PPP	Winsock stack

MATCHING EXERCISE

Match each of the terms with the definitions on the right:

TERMS	DEFINITIONS
1. protocol	**a.** An Internet address in numeric form
2. TCP/IP	**b.** A set of commands and signals that computers use to communicate
3. IP Address	
4. SLIP	**c.** The set of specifications for the interface between TCP/IP application programs and network drivers
5. shell account	**d.** An Internet access method that connects the user to the Internet through a Unix host computer
6. client	
7. Winsock	**e.** The set of protocols that computers use to exchange data through the Internet
8. log in	**f.** A protocol used to connect a computer to the Internet through the computer's serial port
9. e-mail address	
10. Domain Name Server	**g.** A database used to convert from Internet addresses in DNS format to IP addresses
	h. A computer or program that requests information or services through a network
	i. The unique identity of an Internet user
	j. The process of starting a session on a computer by sending the computer the user's name and password

COMPLETION EXERCISE

Fill in the missing word or phrase for each of the following statements:

1. A set of signals and commands is called a _____.

2. Every computer on the Internet has a unique _____.

3. Numeric Internet addresses are called _____ addresses.

4. .edu, .com, and .org are _____.

5. Individual users have Internet addresses in the form _____.

6. A _____ account connects a computer directly to the Internet.

7. A remote terminal connection to the Internet is called a _____ account.

8. The _____ standard defines the interface between application programs and network drivers.

9. A computer that supplies services to a client is called a _____.

10. The Internet service used to connect to a distant computer as a remote terminal is called _____.

SHORT-ANSWER QUESTIONS

Write a brief answer to each of the following questions:

1. Who created the original system that grew into the Internet?

2. What kind of address is *julie@control.com*?

3. What is a Winsock stack?

4. What do you call a program that supplies services to a client?

5. What is the most common activity on the Internet?

6. Name the Internet tool that moves files between computers.

7. What is UUCP?

8. What does an IP address look like?

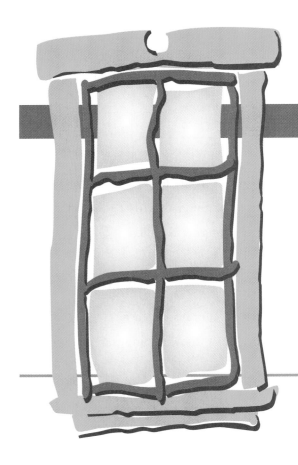

LESSON 2

SENDING AND
RECEIVING E-MAIL

OBJECTIVES

After completing this lesson, you will be able to do the following:

- *Understand how the Internet handles electronic mail.*
- *Configure the Eudora mail manager program.*
- *Write and send electronic mail messages through the Internet.*
- *Receive and file electronic mail from other people.*
- *Use signature blocks and nicknames.*
- *Send electronic mail through the Internet to other online services, including MCI Mail, CompuServe, and America Online.*

CONTENTS

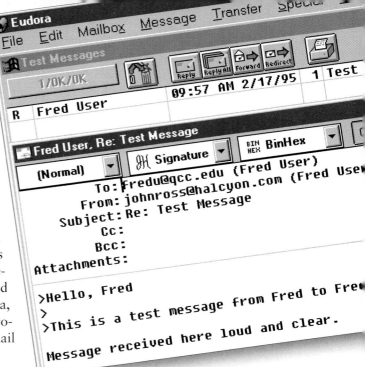

As you learned in Lesson 1, the Internet connects thousands of networks and millions of computers. Electronic mail, also called e-mail, is the single most widely-used Internet service.

In this lesson, you will learn how the Internet handles e-mail, and how to send and receive your own messages and files via e-mail. You'll use Eudora, a freeware mail manager program, to send and receive mail through the Internet.

HOW E-MAIL WORKS

e-mail The exchange of messages and computer files through the Internet and other electronic data networks. Short for "electronic mail."

store-and-forward The process of holding messages on a host and transferring them to their ultimate destination.

mail server A computer that processes electronic mail for client computers.

For a user, the Internet's electronic mail handling system, or **e-mail**, is not difficult: you give the computer the name and address of the person to whom you want to send a message; and then, anywhere from a few minutes to a few hours later, "You have new mail" appears on their screen. Of course, it's not really that simple; there's a lot of internal routing, switching, and traffic management that takes place between the sender and the receiver. It's similar to the way you can dial your aunt's telephone number and be reasonably confident that the telephone in her kitchen will ring, even if you don't know anything about telephone network operation. You can send messages to almost anybody with an e-mail account without knowing the internal details of Internet message handling, as long as you're familiar with e-mail address conventions.

It's important to understand that Internet e-mail is not a way to conduct a live conversation with another user. The recipient of your message will not see your keystrokes at the same time that you type them. Instead, e-mail is a **store-and-forward** system: when you send a message, that message moves from your computer to a post office server, which passes it along through the Internet until it reaches its destination. Eventually, the message arrives at another computer called a **mail server** that holds mail in a mailbox until the recipient retrieves it.

In order to send or receive e-mail, you need a mail handling program. If you have a shell account, the mail program runs on your Internet host. If you have either a direct TCP/IP connection to the Internet or a UUCP account, you must run the mail program on your PC. Either way, the mail program performs these functions:

- It retrieves inbound mail from your local mail server.
- It stores copies of messages that you have sent and received.
- It allows you to compose new messages.
- It sends outbound messages to a post office server.

Most mail programs include additional features, but they'll all include these four.

When you send a letter through the postal system, the address tells the post office where to deliver it. In an e-mail message, the address you provide does the same thing. Every e-mail message has a block of information at the top called a **header**. The header has a "To:" line that includes both the name of the intended recipient and the computer that receives that person's mail.

header A block of information about an e-mail message that appears at the top of the message.

For instance, if you want to send a message to the President of the United States, you would address it as *president@whitehouse.gov*. The DNS address *president@whitehouse.gov* instructs mail-handling computers along the way to forward messages to a computer in the White House. Every e-mail message must have both a complete Internet address and the name of a specific recipient at that address.

STARTING EUDORA

Eudora is a Windows-based program that simplifies creating, sending, receiving, and storing e-mail. The free version of Eudora is limited to Winsock-compliant, direct connections to the Internet. There's also an inexpensive commercial version of Eudora that includes several additional features, including access through a Unix shell account. You can find more information about ordering the commercial version by choosing the About Commercial Eudora command from the Eudora Help menu, which appears in Figure 2-1.

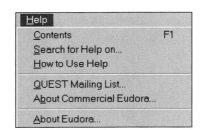

FIGURE 2-1
The Eudora Help menu

In this section, you will create a sample e-mail message, send it to yourself through the Internet, receive the same message, and store the received message on your hard disk.

N O T E   *In order to perform the step-by-step exercises in this chapter, you need a TCP/IP connection to the Internet.*

This lesson assumes that you are running Eudora in Windows 95, which is shown in all screen examples in figures. If you are using Windows 3.1, your screen will look slightly different, but all the steps for using the program will be the same.

LAUNCHING EUDORA

WINDOWS 3.1

HANDS ON

1. Find and open the program group that contains the Eudora icon.

If you don't know where it is, or can't find it, ask your instructor or lab assistant.

2. Double-click on the Eudora icon.

WINDOWS 95

HANDS ON

1. Click once on the Start button, move your cursor to the **Programs** item in the Startup menu, and choose the **Internet Tools** group (or whatever program group contains Eudora) from the Program menu.

2. Select the **Shortcut To Eudora** item from the program group menu.

Figure 2-2 shows the sequence of menus.

FIGURE 2-2
*The Windows 95
Internet Tools menu*

CONFIGURING EUDORA

Before you can use Eudora to send or receive e-mail, you must enter some information about your Internet connection and the way Eudora displays information on your screen.

HANDS ON

1. Open the Special menu and choose **Configuration....**

The dialog box in Figure 2-3 appears.

Your instructor or lab assistant will tell you your e-mail address. The address will be in the format *name@address.edu.*

2. Move your cursor to the **POP Account** field and type your e-mail address in this field.

POP stands for Post Office Protocol. It's the set of rules the mail server uses to store and forward your messages.

3. Type your name in the **Real Name** field.

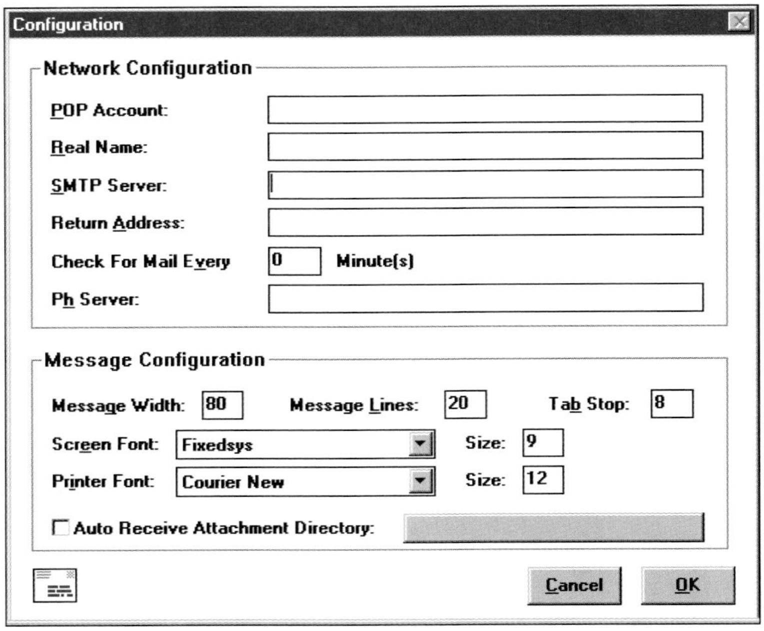

FIGURE 2-3

*The Eudora Configuration
dialog box*

Eudora will include your name in the "From:" line of your message headers.

For the next step, ask your instructor or lab assistant for the name of the Simple Mail Transfer Protocol server that handles mail for your classroom network.

4. Type the name in the **SMTP Server** field.

If a recipient of a message wants to send a reply, he will send it to the return address in the original message. For this exercise, leave the **Return Address** field blank. Eudora will automatically use the name and address in the POP Account field.

The **Check For Mail Every** field specifies how often (in minutes) Eudora will automatically connect to the Post Office Protocol (POP 3) server to see if any new mail has arrived for you. It is set to the default value of 0. For this exercise, don't change it, since you will manually check for new mail.

Leave the **Ph Server** field blank.

The information in the Message Configuration section changes the way Eudora displays and prints messages. You can leave them all at the default settings. However, your messages will be easier to read if you change the Screen Font.

5. Choose **Fixedsys** from the Screen Font menu.

6. Change the number in the **Size** field from 9 to **10**

When you have filled in all the fields on the Configuration dialog box, it will look something like Figure 2-4.

7. Click the OK button to save your configuration.

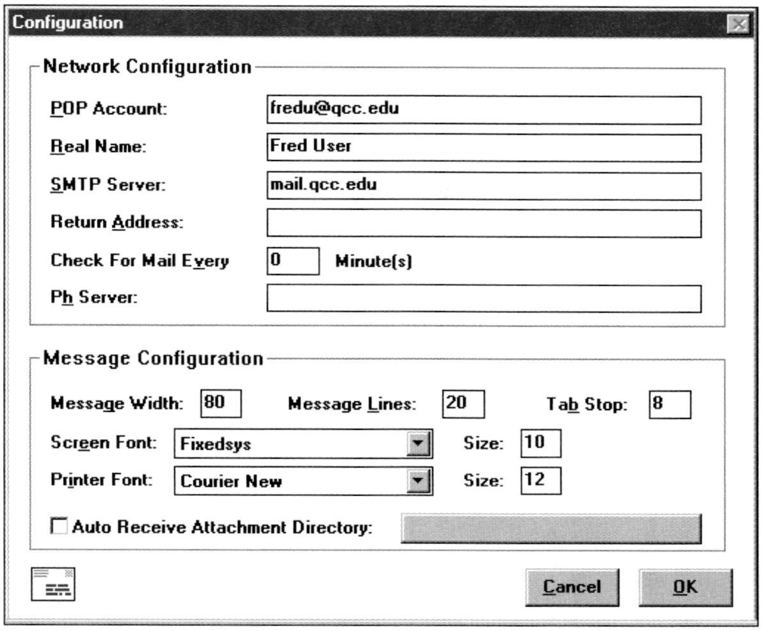

FIGURE 2-4

The Configuration dialog box with names filled in

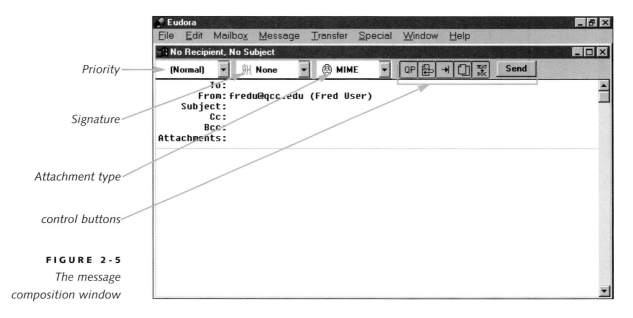

CREATING AND SENDING A MESSAGE

Now you're ready to create your first e-mail message using Eudora. To display the message composition window, open the Message menu and select New Message.

THE MESSAGE COMPOSITION WINDOW TOOLBAR

The toolbar in the message composition window shown in Figure 2-5 includes three drop-down menus and six control buttons.

FIGURE 2-5

The message composition window

- Priority. The Priority box shows the priority of the current message. Unless your network has some kind of in-house system for handling priorities, you should use Normal priority.

- Signature. The Signature box specifies whether or not Eudora will automatically attach a signature block to your message.

- Attachment Type. The Attachment box specifies the way Eudora encodes files that you attach to your message. You will learn how to attach files to messages later in this lesson.

The six control buttons are push-on/push-off. When you click on a button, it will change from off to on or on to off. When a button has a shadow around it, so it looks like it is "pushed down," it's on.

- Quoted-Printable Encoding. When Quoted-Printable Encoding is on, Eudora replaces special characters (such as those used in non-English text) in MIME-encoded files with an equal sign (=), and it makes some other minor changes that make those files easier to read. Unless you learn that the recipient is having trouble reading the files you send, you should leave Quoted-Printable Encoding on.

- Word Wrap. When Word Wrap is on, Eudora automatically adds line breaks when a line of characters is longer than 80 characters. You should keep Word Wrap on to avoid having text run off the right side of your screen.

- Tabs. When the Tabs button is on, and the cursor is in the body of your message, the cursor will move to the next tab stop when you press (Tab) on your keyboard. When the Tabs button is off, pressing (Tab) will move the cursor to the "To:" field in the message header.

- Keep Copy. When the Keep Copy button is on, Eudora keeps copies of all outgoing messages in your Out mailbox after it sends them. When Keep Copy is off, Eudora discards messages after they have been sent. It's a good idea to keep this option on.

- Text As Document. When Text As Document is on, Eudora sends text files attached to messages as separate document files. When it is off, attached text files become part of the message itself.

- Send. When you click the Send button, Eudora transmits the current message to the Internet.

Here's how to compose and send a message:

HANDS ON

1. Select **New Message** from the Message menu.

The message composition window in Figure 2-6 appears.

Notice that Eudora automatically enters your name and address in the From field.

The To field identifies the person who will receive a message.

2. Since you're sending this message to yourself, type your own e-mail address in the **To** field.

3. Press (Tab) to move the cursor to the **Subject** field.

message composition toolbar →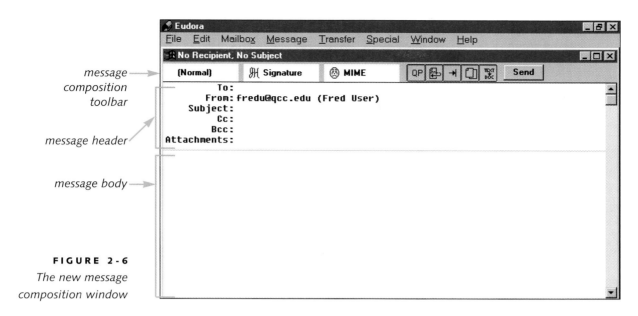

message header →

message body →

FIGURE 2-6
The new message composition window

4. Type **Test Message** in this field.

The Cc (carbon copy) and Bcc (blind carbon copy) fields are for additional names and addresses of people to whom you want to send "for your information" copies of a message. Leave them blank.

5. Press Tab until the cursor is in the lower part of the message composition window.

6. Type the text of your message.

The message doesn't have to be very long, since you're sending it to yourself. If you make a typing error, you can use the arrow keys or your mouse to move back and correct something you've already typed.

Figure 2-7 shows a filled-in message.

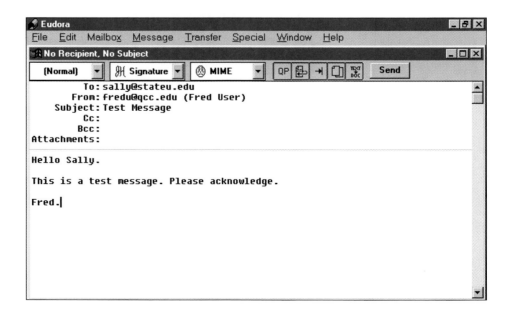

FIGURE 2-7
A short message in the message composition window

7. When the text of the message is complete, click the Send button in the toolbar.

When you click the Send button, Eudora connects to the Internet, the window closes, and the Progress window, shown in Figure 2-8, appears on your screen. The Progress window tells you that Eudora is transferring the message to your network's outbound mail server, which will pass it along to the recipient.

FIGURE 2-8

The Progress window

RECEIVING A MESSAGE

When somebody sends you an e-mail message, that message goes to your POP (Post Office Protocol) server. Eudora can check for new mail either on a pre-arranged schedule, or in response to a command. In the previous section, you sent a message to yourself; in this section, you will receive that message from the Internet.

MANUALLY CHECKING FOR MAIL

Follow these steps to manually download your mail from the POP server:

HANDS ON

1. Choose the **Check Mail** command from the File menu.

The Enter Password dialog box in Figure 2-9 will appear.

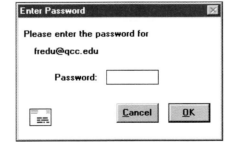

FIGURE 2-9

The Enter Password dialog box

2. Type the password provided by your instructor.

Eudora will not display your password, but it will show an asterisk (*) for each character you type.

3. Click the OK button.

If your message has arrived, Eudora will display a series of progress screens, followed by the "You have new mail" message shown in Figure 2-10.

FIGURE 2-10

The new mail information window

NOTE | *If your message has not yet arrived, try again (starting with Step 1) until you receive it.*

4. Click the OK button to close the "You have new mail" information window.

RECEIVING MAIL AUTOMATICALLY

In addition to manual mail retrieval, Eudora can also contact the mail server on a regular schedule and notify you when it receives new mail. Follow these steps to set up an automatic mail retrieval schedule:

HANDS ON

1. Choose the **Configuration** command from the Special menu.

A dialog box that contains the section shown in Figure 2-11 appears.

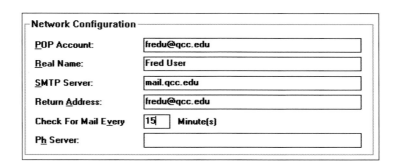

FIGURE 2-11

Fill in the Check For Mail Every field

2. In the **Check For Mail Every** field, type **15**

3. Click the OK button to save the changes and close the Configuration dialog box.

READING NEW MAIL

Inbox A Eudora file that contains inbound e-mail messages.

When Eudora receives a new message, it stores it in a mailbox called the **Inbox**. To read a new message, follow these steps:

HANDS ON

1. Choose Mailbox, **In**. In other words, choose the **In** command from Mailbox menu.

The In mailbox window in Figure 2-12 will appear, with information about your test message. Notice that there's a dot in the left-hand column. This indicates that you have not yet read this message.

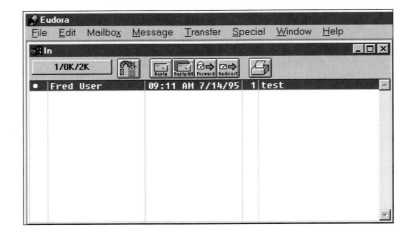

FIGURE 2-12

The In mailbox window with one new message

2. Double-click on the message description to see its contents.

Figure 2-13 shows a received message.

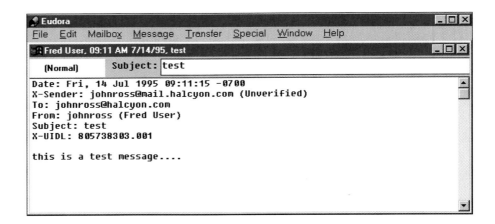

FIGURE 2-13

A received message

3. To close the message window, click on the Close button in the title bar of the window. Be sure you don't click the button in the title bar of the larger Eudora window or you will shut down the program.

THE MAILBOX TOOLBAR BUTTONS

mailbox A storage area on a mail server where the server holds mail for an individual address until that subscriber's mail program downloads it.

Eudora stores inbound and outbound messages in folders called **mailboxes**. A single mailbox may contain any number of separate messages.

When you delete a message from a mailbox by clicking on the Trash button, Eudora holds the deleted message in a special mailbox called Trash. To completely remove messages from your disk, use the Empty Trash command in the Special menu. If the "Empty Trash on Quit" option in the Switches dialog is active, Eudora also cleans out the Trash mailbox when you shut down the program.

Mailbox windows and windows that contain received messages have a toolbar with seven control buttons:

- Mailbox Size. The Mailbox Size button has three numbers in it. Starting at the left, the first number shows the number of messages in this mailbox. The second number is the amount of space these messages occupy on your disk, and the third is the amount of wasted space in this mailbox.

  When you click on the Mailbox Size button, Eudora recovers the wasted space. The Compact Mailboxes command in the Special menu recovers wasted space from all mailboxes at one time. If you don't recover wasted space manually, Eudora will eventually do so automatically.

- Trash. The Trash button moves all currently highlighted messages to the Trash mailbox.

- Reply. The Reply button creates a reply to the currently highlighted message, and addresses it to the person who sent the original message. The reply includes the text of the original message, with a ">" symbol at the beginning of each line.

- Reply All. The Reply All button creates a reply to the currently highlighted message, and addresses it to the person who sent the original message and to all other recipients of the original message.

- Forward. The Forward button copies the header and text of the currently highlighted message into a new message, with a ">" symbol at the beginning of each line. To send a forwarded message, you must fill in the name and address of the recipient. You can also add your own comments to the text.

- Redirect. The Redirect button copies the text of the currently highlighted message to a new message. To send a redirected message, you must fill in the name and address of the new recipient. You can also add new text or edit the original message. Unlike the Forward command, Redirect does not show the original header or add a ">" symbol to each line.

- Print. The Print button sends the currently highlighted message to your printer.

USING THE MESSAGE QUEUE

Rather than sending each message as your write it, you can also use Eudora to hold your messages and send them as a group. This is called a **message queue**. If you have a dial-in connection to the Internet, queuing your e-mail might be less costly, because you don't have to go online (connect to the Internet) until after you have composed all of your messages.

To use message queuing, you open the Switches dialog box by selecting the Switches command in the Special menu. When the Switches dialog box appears, turn off the Immediate Send option.

To send queued messages, open the File menu and select the Send Queued Messages command.

message queue A "holding area" for messages that Eudora or another mail manager program will upload to a mail server when a connection is established.

STORING YOUR MESSAGES

After you send or receive a message, you may want to keep a copy on your hard drive for future reference. Eudora includes a set of mailboxes to organize the way it holds messages. You can see a list of mailboxes by opening the Mailbox menu.

When you first run Eudora, it has just three mailboxes: In, Out and Trash. The Inbox contains received messages, the Outbox contains messages that you have sent to other people, and the Trashbox contains messages that you deleted from other mailboxes. If you want to sort your messages by subject, by sender or recipient, or by date, you can create as many additional mailboxes as you want, and transfer messages from the in- or outbox to any of the others.

Follow these steps to create a new mailbox and transfer a message:

HANDS ON

1. Choose the **In** command from the Mailbox menu.

The In mailbox, as shown in Figure 2-14, contains one item, a message from you.

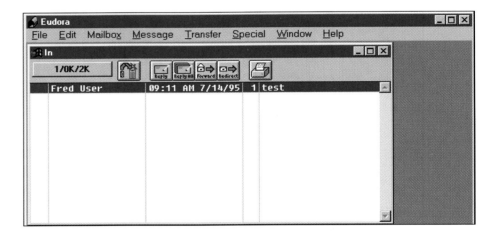

FIGURE 2-14
The In mailbox

2. Click on the message listing to highlight it.

3. Choose **New** from the Transfer menu.

The New Mailbox Dialog in Figure 2-15 appears.

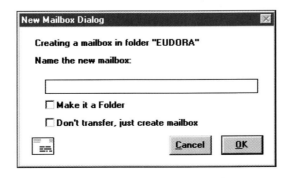

FIGURE 2-15
The New Mailbox Dialog

4. Type **Test Messages** in the **Name** field and click the OK button.

Notice that the message listing has disappeared from the In mailbox.

5. Select the **Test Messages** command from the Mailbox menu.

The new Test Messages mailbox window is open, with your message on the first line of the message list. Figure 2-16 shows the new Test Messages window.

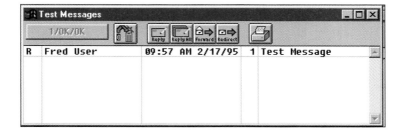

FIGURE 2-16

The newly created Test Messages mailbox

If you prefer, you can create folders that contain your new mailboxes. When you create a new folder, Eudora places it in a subdirectory under the main program directory. A folder may contain an unlimited number of separate mailboxes.

SENDING A REPLY TO A MESSAGE

When you receive an e-mail message, you will often want to send an answer back to the person who sent the original message to you. You could create a new message, but Eudora offers an easier method. The Reply function automatically quotes the original message and fills in your name and address in the "From:" field of the message header.

Pretend for a moment that the message you just received was from somebody else, and that you want to reply to it.

HANDS ON

1. With your Test Messages mailbox open, highlight the listing for the test message you sent earlier.

2. Click the Reply button in the Mailbox toolbar.

A message composition window appears with the header already filled in, and the text of the original message in the body of the message with a ">" symbol at the beginning of each line, as shown in Figure 2-17.

You can edit this message just as you would a new message. It frequently makes it easier for the sender of the original message to follow the thread of the conversation when you include a copy of their question in the text of your reply. For a long message, instead of quoting the entire message, you can quote only parts, like the beginning and end, or the main question—enough to give the sender an idea of what you're replying to. When you have edited the message to your satisfaction, you're ready to transmit it.

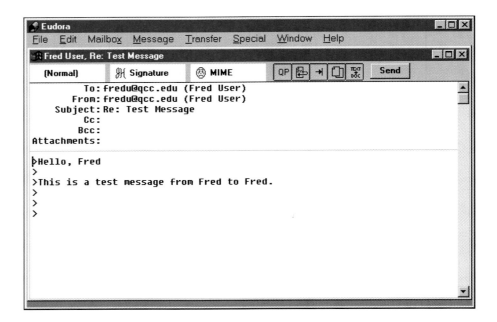

FIGURE 2-17

A quoted message in a new window

3. Click the Send or Queue button to transmit the message.

USING MESSAGE HEADERS

Every e-mail message has a header that contains information about that message, including the date, originator, destination, and subject. The Internet mail system uses this information to route your message through the Internet to its recipient.

Many of the fields in a message header are important to the mail-handling system, but not particularly significant to most readers.

Unless you're trying to analyze the way a message got from the sender to its destination, there are really only a few sections of each header that matter: the Date, To, From, and Subject lines. Therefore, Eudora allows you to hide all the other parts of a header.

Follow these steps to expand or compact the message headers you see in Eudora:

HANDS ON

1. From the Special menu, select **Switches**.

The first item in the Miscellany box in the right column is Show All Headers.

2. If there is not a check mark next to **Show All Headers,** click on it to make it active.

3. Click the OK button to save your choice and close the dialog box.

4. Select Mailbox, **Test Messages** to open your Test Messages mailbox.

5. Double-click on the message description for the message you sent to yourself.

A message window appears. Notice that the message header has about a dozen lines of information. Figure 2-18 shows a message with a complete header.

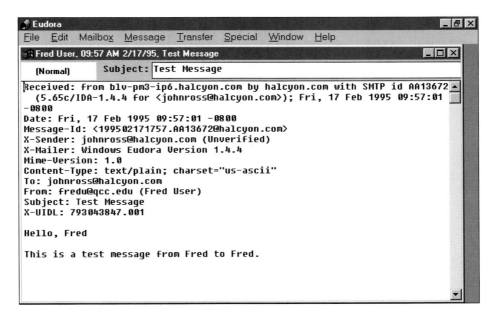

FIGURE 2-18

A message with the entire header visible

6. Click the Close button in the upper-right corner of the message window to close it. (Don't close the Eudora window by mistake.)

7. Select Special, **Switches** to open the Switches dialog box again.

8. This time, click **Show All Headers** in the Miscellany box to turn this option off.

9. Click the OK button to save the change and close the dialog box. The Test Messages mailbox window should still be visible.

10. Double-click the same message description you opened in Step 5.

The message window opens again, but the message header should only contain about half a dozen lines. Most of the least interesting fields are now hidden. Figure 2-19 shows a test message with a compacted header.

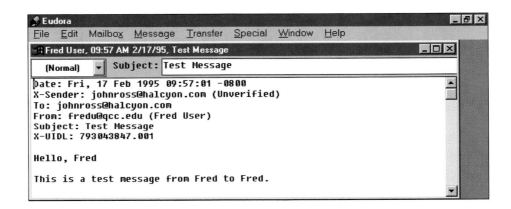

FIGURE 2-19

The same message with unimportant parts of the header hidden

USING SIGNATURE BLOCKS

signature block A standard block of text at the end of an e-mail message or news article that contains information about the person who originated the message.

Many e-mail users add a **signature block** at the end of each message, including the sender's name, their e-mail address, and possibly some alternative methods for making contact, such as a voice telephone number or a postal address. The name and address in a message header doesn't always convey much useful information (the Internet may know that *fredu@qcc.edu* is Fred User at Quaker Community College, but a human reader doesn't). A signature block is a useful way to let people who receive e-mail know who sent it to them.

TIP   *Some people have incredibly elaborate signature blocks that include quotations from their favorite television shows, expressions of their political or social philosophy, or cartoons constructed from ASCII characters. These extended signature blocks may be amusing the first time you see them, but they're really not a good idea. After about the third time you receive a four-line message with a 17-line signature, the signature loses its entertainment value.*

Eudora can automatically add a standard signature block to every message you send. Follow these steps to create your signature block:

HANDS ON

1. Select Window, **Signature**.

The Signature window as shown in Figure 2-20 will appear.

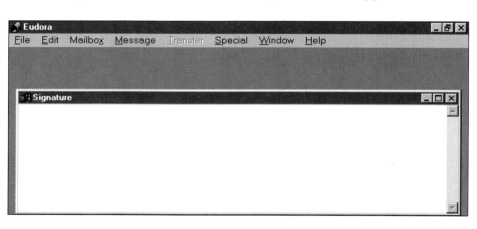

FIGURE 2-20

A new Signature window

2. Type your signature block in the Signature window.

In general, it's best to limit your signature to about four lines. Figure 2-21 shows a typical signature block.

3. When you're happy with your signature block, select the **Save** command from the File menu.

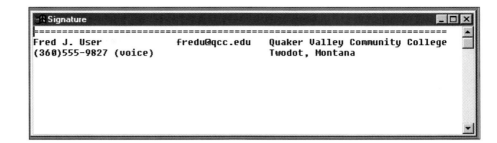

FIGURE 2-21

A signature block in the Signature window

To automatically attach your signature block at the end of every message, select the Signature option in the composition window toolbar.

4. Close the Signature window.

ATTACHING FILES TO MESSAGES

In addition to simple text, you can also use e-mail to send and receive files by attaching them to messages. This is a handy way to move programs and data files across the Internet.

An attached file is not part of the message it accompanies, but it travels through the Internet with it. There's an "Attachments" field in the message header that identifies the name of the attached file, as shown in Figure 2-22.

```
        To: sallyw@stateu.edu
      From: fredu@qcc.edu (Fred User)
   Subject: Test Message with Attachment
        Cc:
       Bcc:
Attachments: C:\INET_PT\EUDORA\EUDORA.INI;
```

FIGURE 2-22

A message header with an attachment

SENDING A MESSAGE WITH AN ATTACHMENT

In this section, you will use Eudora to create a message with an attached file and send it to yourself.

HANDS ON

1. Open the Message menu and select the **New Message** command.

A new message window will appear.

2. Type your own e-mail address in the **To** field.

3. Press Tab to move to the **Subject** field. Type **Test with Attachment**

4. Press Tab three times to move the cursor to the body of your message.

Notice that the cursor skips over the Attachments field.

5. Type a brief message to yourself.

6. Select the **Attach Document** command from the Message menu.

The Attach Document dialog box, as shown in Figure 2-23, will appear.

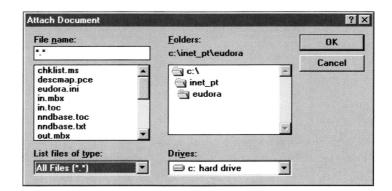

FIGURE 2-23
*The Attach Document
file browser*

7. Use the file browser in the Attach Document dialog box to highlight the **eudora.ini** file and then click the OK button.

Notice that Attachments field now shows the full path of the **eudora.ini** file.

8. Click on the Send button to transmit the file.

RECEIVING A MESSAGE WITH AN ATTACHMENT

Now you will use Eudora to receive the file you sent in the previous section.

HANDS
ON

1. Select File, **Check Mail.**

When Eudora connects to the mail server, it will transfer your waiting mail to your PC. The Save Attachment dialog box appears, as shown in Figure 2-24.

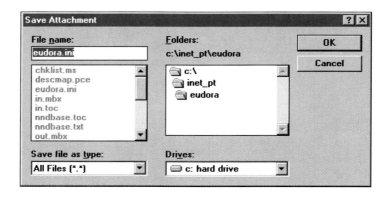

FIGURE 2-24
*The Save Attachment
file browser*

2. Select the **C:** folder and click the OK button.

The Progress window will tell you that Eudora is transferring the file. Eudora automatically places the newly received message in your Inbox.

3. When the "You have new mail." message appears, click the OK button.

Now you'll check to see that there's a copy of the **eudora.ini** file in your **C:** directory.

4. Open the **Windows Explorer** in Windows 95, or open the **File Manager** in Windows 3.1.

Since you won't need the copy of the eudora.ini file, you'll delete it.

5. Look in the **C:** directory to locate the **eudora.ini** file and delete it.

USING ADDRESS BOOKS AND ALIASES

E-mail addresses are fine for computers, but it can be really tedious to type the same string of characters every time you send somebody a message. This is especially true if you want to send a message to somebody with a complicated address, such as *susan@evolution.genetics.washington.edu.*

Rather than typing the full e-mail name and address every time you compose a new message to one of your regular correspondents, you can create an easy-to-remember alias, such as a first name, full name or initials. For example, you might use "susan" as the alias for that long e-mail address. An **alias** is a substitute for one or more e-mail addresses. Eudora calls aliases **nicknames**.

alias A short name that identifies one or more e-mail addresses.

nickname An alias in Eudora.

TIP   *You can also use an alias to automatically send the same message to more than one person. For example, you might create an alias called "sales department" that sends bulletins to sales people in all of your company's branch offices.*

CREATING A NICKNAME FROM SCRATCH

Suppose you want to assign a nickname to an e-mail address for someone in your computer class, so you don't have to remember the exact e-mail address.

HANDS ON

1. Select the **Nicknames** command from the Window menu.

The Nicknames dialog box appears, as shown in Figure 2-25.

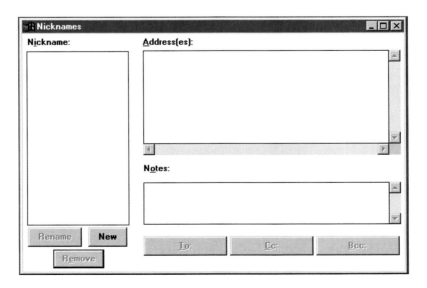

FIGURE 2-25

The Nicknames window as it first appears

2. Click the New button.

The New Nickname dialog box, as shown in Figure 2-26 appears.

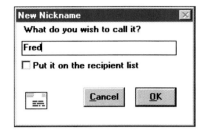

FIGURE 2-26
*The New Nickname
dialog box*

3. Type your friend's first name.

4. Since you want this nickname to also appear in the Quick Recipient list under the Message menu, make the **Put It On The Recipient List** option active.

5. Move the cursor to the **Address(es)** box and type your friend's Internet e-mail addresses.

You may also type this person's full name in parentheses.

6. Press Tab to move your cursor to the **Notes** box.

You can use Notes to record additional information about a nickname, such as that person's title or full name and maybe an alternative method of reaching him. If you prefer, you can leave the Notes box empty.

Figure 2-27 shows a filled-in Nicknames dialog box.

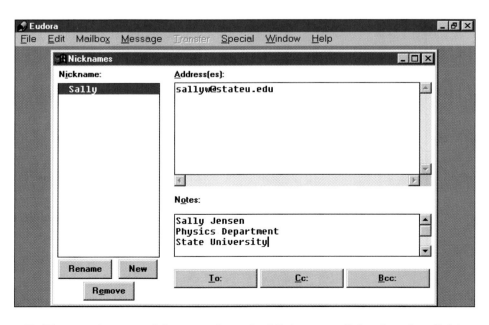

FIGURE 2-27
*The Nicknames window
with a nickname filled in*

7. To save the new nickname, close the Nicknames dialog box by clicking the X button in the upper-right corner.

USING A NICKNAME TO ADDRESS A MESSAGE

Once you have created a nickname, you can use it to send messages to the name or names assigned to that nickname. There are several ways to do this:

- Type the nickname in the To, Cc, or Bcc field of the message header.

- Open the Nicknames window, highlight a nickname and click on the To, Cc, or Bcc button.

- Choose a nickname from the New Message To submenu under the Message menu.

SENDING E-MAIL TO PEOPLE ON OTHER SERVICES

The Internet itself is huge, but it is also connected through gateways to just about every other public (and most private) electronic mail system in the world. Even if somebody is not "on the Internet," you can probably exchange e-mail with him, if you know his e-mail address.

Most of the time, people will give you their e-mail address in Internet format—the familiar *name@address.xxx*. But sometimes they will tell you an address in the format they use on their own service, such as *78721,999* or *FredU7234*. As a rule of thumb, if the address doesn't have an @ in it, the Internet won't recognize it.

Here's how to convert e-mail addresses from other services to Internet addresses:

- CompuServe. CompuServe Information Service (CIS) uses number addresses, with a comma in the middle. To convert to an Internet address, change the comma to a period and add *@compuserve.com* to the end. For example, to send mail to a CIS subscriber with the address *78721,999*, this would be the correct Internet address to use: *78721.999@compuserve.com*.

- America Online. America Online subscribers' addresses may be either names or combinations of names and numbers. To convert to an Internet address, add *@aol.com* to the end. For example, to send mail to *FredU7234*, use this Internet address: *fredu7234@aol.com*.

- MCI Mail. MCI Mail subscribers have both a user name and an address that looks like a telephone number. To convert to an Internet address, you can use either the name or number followed by *@mcimail.com*. However, many common names identify more than one account, so you should use the number whenever possible. For example, if Susan Collins has MCI Mail number *234-5678*, her best Internet address would be *2345678@mcimail.com*.

Almost every other gateway either uses the standard *name@address.xxx* format. For example, to send mail to Fred User, who subscribes to Prodigy, you would use *fredu@prodigy.com*. There are a few exceptions, but the people using those services will generally give you their addresses in Internet format.

LESSON SUMMARY AND EXERCISES

After completing this lesson, you should know how to do the following:

HOW E-MAIL WORKS

- E-mail is a store-and-forward system.
- Every message includes a header with the destination and other essential information.

STARTING EUDORA

- To start Eudora, click on the Eudora icon.
- To configure Eudora, use the Configuration dialog box.

CREATING AND SENDING A MESSAGE

- To create a message in Eudora, select New Message in the Message menu and type the text in the message composition window.
- To transmit the message, click on the Send button.

RECEIVING A MESSAGE

- To receive incoming e-mail messages in Eudora, select the Check Mail command in the File menu.

READING NEW MAIL

- To read new messages in Eudora, use the In command from the Mailbox menu, and double-click on message listings with a dot in the left-hand column.

SENDING A REPLY TO A MESSAGE

- To reply to a message in Eudora, display the message and choose the Reply command in the Message menu.
- Type the text of your reply in the message composition window.

USING MESSAGE HEADERS

- Message headers contain information the Internet uses to deliver each message, including the date, originator, destination, and subject.

USING SIGNATURE BLOCKS

- A signature block is an optional block of text that some people add to the end of every e-mail message they send.
- A signature block may contain a name and return address, a quotation or closing lines, or a block of useful information.

ATTACHING FILES TO MESSAGES

- An e-mail message may have a data file or program file attached to it.
- To attach a file using Eudora, use the Attach Document command in the Message menu.

USING ADDRESS BOOKS AND ALIASES

- To assign an alias in Eudora, use the Nicknames command in the Window menu.

SENDING E-MAIL TO PEOPLE ON OTHER SERVICES

- To send e-mail to other online services, use this address format: *name@name_of_service.com.*

NEW TERMS TO REMEMBER

After completing this lesson, you should know the meaning of these terms:

alias	mailbox
e-mail	message queue
header	nickname
Inbox	signature block
mail server	store-and-forward

MATCHING EXERCISE

Match each of the terms with the definitions on the right:

TERMS

1. e-mail
2. mail server
3. header
4. POP server
5. Inbox
6. mailbox
7. message queue
8. signature block
9. address
10. attachment

DEFINITIONS

a. A standard block of information about the sender of an e-mail message

b. A file where e-mail messages are stored before the recipient receives them

c. A text file or data file that accompanies an e-mail message

d. A computer that receives mail from the Internet and holds it until the recipient requests it

e. The exchange of messages and files across computer networks

f. The identity of an Internet user

g. A group of messages stored on the user's computer for later relay to the Internet

h. A computer that receives outbound e-mail messages and passes them on to the Internet for delivery

i. A block of information at the top of an e-mail message, including the names and addresses of the originator and recipient

j. The file where Eudora stores newly received messages

COMPLETION EXERCISE

Fill in the missing word or phrase for each of the following statements:

1. A mail manager program retrieves mail from _____ .

2. The name and address of the recipient of an e-mail message appears in the _____ field of the header.

3. Incoming e-mail is stored in the _____ server until you retrieve it.

4. Eudora stores messages in folders called _____ .

5. A signature block should generally be no more than _____ lines.

6. A file sent as part of an e-mail message is called an _____ .

7. To send the same message to more than one recipient, you can use _____ .

8. The destination of an e-mail message is called an _____ .

9. The date and time a message was sent appear in the _____ .

10. To transmit a message in Eudora, click on the _____ button.

SHORT-ANSWER QUESTIONS

Write a brief answer to each of the following questions:

1. To send an e-mail message to Compuserve address *70777,502*, what Internet e-mail address would you use?

2. If somebody asks you a question in an e-mail message, what's the easiest way to answer?

3. How would you move a message to a different Eudora message file?

4. What Eudora command do you use to find out if there are any new messages waiting for you on your mail server?

5. What kind of information should you put in the Subject field of a message header?

APPLICATION PROJECTS

Perform the following actions to complete these projects:

1. Your instructor or lab assistant will tell you his or her e-mail address. Send a message to that address with your name and your answers to the Short-Answer Questions in this lesson.

2. Your instructor or lab assistant will give you a list of e-mail addresses for other members of your class. Send a message to the person at the next computer to your left, asking that person to describe your shoes.

3. When you receive a message from the person to your right, send that person a reply.

4. Create an alias that includes four people in your class and send them a message that includes the following information:

   a. How did you come to class today? Did you drive, walk, or take the bus?

   b. What did you eat for breakfast today?

5. Choose another e-mail address from the list you received from your instructor or lab assistant and send them a message with the *C:\windows\win.ini* file as an attachment.

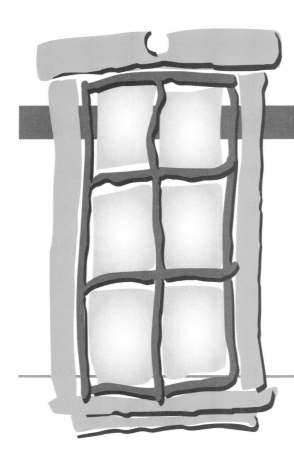

LESSON 3

INTERNET NEWS

OBJECTIVES

After completing this lesson, you will be able to do the following:

- *Understand how Usenet news is organized.*
- *Subscribe to news groups.*
- *Read news articles.*
- *Create and post your own articles in news groups.*
- *Reply to news articles.*

I
n the last lesson, you learned about exchanging messages with other Internet users through e-mail. E-mail is fine for private one-to-one communication, but when you want to reach a lot of people with the same message, posting a public announcement on the Internet equivalent of a bulletin board is a better approach. One of the most popular features of the Internet is **news**, which distributes public messages to people around the world.

	106	FAQ on ma
Britt Klein	34	Re: LONGE
Louis Nick	350	Re: How to
Byron Uytiepo	14	Re: test ar
RHirsh	22	Re: test
Raymond Steven Kutai	11	Re: How
The Baron	26	Re: How
DaveHatunen	18	Re: Inter
Nam Pham	17	Re: How
Andrew Ostergren	64	Re: whi
RHirsh	15	Netsca
RHirsh	11	
Luke Taylor		

A large and varied amount of material moves around the Internet as news. News ranges from discussions of popular television shows to announcements of new developments in every imaginable academic discipline, and from requests for help repairing seventy-year-old radios to information about the latest activities in artificial intelligence. In order to allow people to find the things they want and ignore the others, Internet news is sorted into thousands of separate topics, called **news groups**. Some popular news groups might include hundreds of new messages every day, while other news groups devoted to more obscure subjects might handle only three or four messages a week.

Many news groups are distributed worldwide through a system called **Usenet**. Others are limited to a smaller geographical region, or to specific private networks or commercial services. Usenet originally used a store-and-forward process, called UUCP (Unix to Unix CoPy) to pass news packets through dial-up telephone connections. Some Usenet users still use UUCP to obtain their news feeds, but today, Usenet news groups are distributed to UUCP hosts through the Internet.

With a few exceptions, news groups are co-operative services that do not have any formal administrators. Anybody can post a message called an **article** that will be distributed to all the other subscribers of that news group. The exceptions are **moderated news groups**, in which all articles are reviewed by a person who screens for content appropriate to the topic before releasing them to the network.

In order to read and contribute to news groups on the Internet, you must use a program called a **news reader**, which obtains news articles from a computer called a **news server**. In this lesson, you will use a news reader called Trumpet, but the general principles are the same for any other news reader you might see.

news The electronic exchange of public messages organized by subject.

news group A set of news articles about a single topic.

Usenet The most formally organized part of the worldwide electronic exchange of news groups. Usenet messages are distributed through the Internet and other electronic information exchange systems.

article A message posted to a news group.

moderated news group A news group whose messages are reviewed by a "host" or "moderator" to assure that all messages are related to the news group's topic.

news reader An application program for sending and receiving online news articles.

news server A computer that supplies news articles to a news reader program.

HOW INTERNET NEWS IS ORGANIZED

Within the universe of Internet News, there are more than 7,000 separate news groups. The name of each group identifies the subject under discussion, and the major category within which this particular subject falls. Words within a news group's name are separated by periods, just like domain names.

As a general rule, the first word (or abbreviation) of a news group's name is the broad general classification, and each additional word in the name is more specific. So within the major "rec" (for recreational) group, there's a subgroup called "*rec.food*," which includes separate news groups devoted to recipes, restaurants, and so forth. Some of these groups are themselves broken into still smaller groups; in addition to *rec.food.drink*, there are also separate news groups called *rec.food.drink.tea* and *rec.food.drink.coffee*.

You may see as many as two hundred different "major" news group categories, including regional headings (such as *atl* for Atlanta or *nz* for New Zealand), institutional headings (such as *yale*), and headings that describe individual network services such as *netcom* or *uunet*. But the most widely distributed news groups fall under the seven major Usenet categories and a handful of "alternative" categories.

The seven Usenet categories are:

comp	Computer-related topics
news	Topics related to Usenet news
rec	Hobbies, arts, and recreational activities
sci	Science and technology (except computers)
soc	Social issues and politics
talk	Debates, and controversies
misc	Topics that don't fit one of the other categories

The important alternative categories include:

alt	A catch-all for "alternative" news groups. Some are too unconventional for one of the Usenet categories (*alt.alien.visitors*, *alt.happy.birthday.to.me*), while in other cases, the originators didn't want to go through the formal approvals needed to set up an official Usenet news group. The *alt* category is about evenly divided between really interesting and completely useless groups.
bionet	News groups related to the biological sciences
biz	News groups on business topics, including advertisements, which are not permitted in other groups
clari	News from the Associated Press and Reuters wire services, supplied through the commercial Clarinet service
k12	News groups for primary and secondary schools teachers and students

netiquette The body of commonly accepted rules for exchange of e-mail and news through the Internet and other electronic networks.

FAQ Frequently Asked Questions. A set of questions and answers that contain introductory information about a specific subject.

Before beginning, you should know about a few commonly-accepted rules and traditions, sometimes called **netiquette**:

■ Before you post a question to a news group, read the articles that other people have posted for at least a week or two. Chances are good that you may see an answer to your own questions.

■ In many news groups, there's a set of answers to "frequently asked questions," called a **FAQ**, that gets posted every few weeks, or maybe once a month. If you ask one of those common questions, you'll probably get several replies advising you to "read the FAQ."

■ Limit your articles to the topic of the news group where you post them. Just because you think some political, social, or other issue is important, that's no reason to talk about it in a news group dedicated to cellular biology.

■ When you're responding to an article, it's helpful to quote a few lines of the original, so other readers will know what you're talking about. Don't quote headers or signature lines.

■ Although it is distributed through private communication services, Usenet is not a commercial service for private users. It may occur to you that there are millions of people reading Usenet news, and if you post a message advertising your business to a couple of hundred news groups, you could find a lot of new customers. *Don't do it!* You will get many people angry at you, you'll receive thousands of really nasty e-mail messages, and your Internet service provider will probably cancel your account. The same thing applies to chain letters and other pyramid schemes.

■ Remember that Internet news goes all around the world. Don't assume that everybody who reads your article shares your own culture and values.

■ Don't believe everything you read in a news group. Just because somebody can figure out how to write and post an article, there's no guarantee that he knows what he's talking about.

CONFIGURING TRUMPET NEWS

The first time you run the Trumpet News Reader program, you must identify yourself and the names of the computers used by your Internet service provider as news and mail servers.

Follow these steps to configure the program:

HANDS ON

1. Turn on the computer.

2. When the Windows 95 Desktop appears, click **Start** to open the Startup menu, and then click **Programs** to open the Program menu.

3. Select **Internet Tools** from the Program menu.

If you're using Windows 3.1, use the Program Manager to open Eudora.

4. Select **Trumpet News** from the Internet Tools menu.

The Trumpet Setup dialog box appears, as shown in Figure 3-1. If you don't see it, click the OK button in the copyright window, and then select the Setup command in the File menu to open the dialog box.

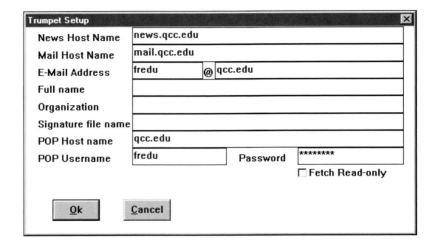

FIGURE 3-1

The Trumpet Setup dialog box

5. Fill in the Setup dialog box with information provided by your instructor.

When installing Trumpet News on a system outside the classroom, you can obtain this information from your network administrator or your Internet service provider's technical support.

6. Click OK.

If Trumpet does not automatically connect to your news server, select the Reconnect command from the File menu.

You only need to configure Trumpet News once. After that, it will automatically connect to your news server as soon as you start the program. When the news reader is connected to a server, the name of the server appears directly under the menu bar, as shown in Figure 3-2.

FIGURE 3-2

The name of the news server appears under the menu bar

 EADING NEWS

Reading news is a two-step process: selecting the news groups you want to see, and choosing individual articles from those news groups.

SUBSCRIBING TO NEWS GROUPS

subscribe The process of joining a news group in order to receive new articles as they appear.

The first step in reading news is to decide which news groups you want to follow. When you **subscribe** to a news group, your news reader will show you a list of articles in that group. In this section, you will use the Trumpet News Reader program to explore your news server's news groups and subscribe to two of them.

To subscribe to news groups in Trumpet News:

1. Choose **Subscribe** from the Group menu. It may take five minutes or more for Trumpet to load all the news groups.

The Subscribe To News Groups dialog box in Figure 3-3 will appear.

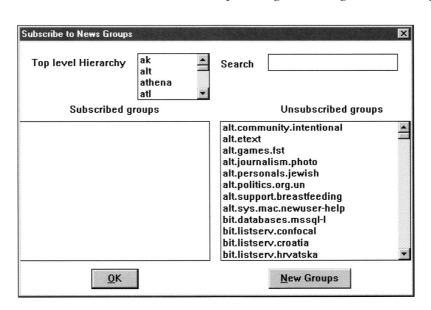

FIGURE 3-3

The Subscribe to News Groups dialog box

2. Scroll down to **alt** using the scroll bar at the right of the **Top Level Hierarchy** box.

A list of news groups will appear in the Unsubscribed Groups box.

3. Click on **alt.test** in the **Unsubscribed Groups** box.

The alt.test group will move to the Subscribed Groups box. Alt.test is a special news group for people who want to test their ability to send and receive messages without filling other news groups with messages that nobody wants to read.

4. Return to the Top Level Hierarchy box and scroll down until the **rec** listing is visible.

5. Click on **rec**.

6. In the **Unsubscribed Groups** box, scroll down until you see **rec.arts.tv**.

7. Click on **rec.arts.tv** to move it to the **Subscribed Groups** box.

8. Click the OK button to close the Subscribe To News Group dialog box.

The top half of the News window shows the two news groups you selected.

9. Double-click on the name of a group to see a list of current messages in that group.

Trumpet News will scan that group for messages you haven't already read, and display a list of articles in the bottom half of the window. Figure 3-4 shows a list of messages.

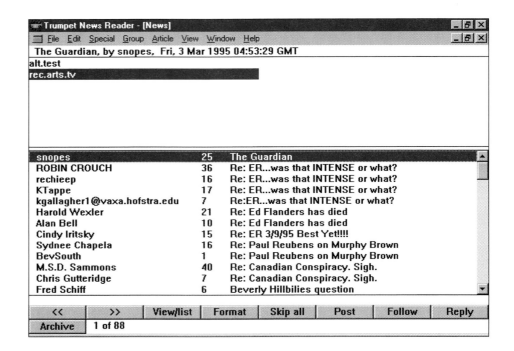

FIGURE 3-4
The list of articles fills the bottom of the subject window

READING ARTICLES IN A NEWS GROUP

Each news group contains a set of messages, called articles related to the news group topic. In this section, you will retrieve news articles from your news server.

HANDS ON

1. Double-click on the listing for the **alt.test** news group.

A Progress window appears while the program scans for new articles. When the scan is complete, a list of new articles will appear in the lower half of the screen. The list will look similar to the one in Figure 3-5, but it will contain a different list of articles.

The list of articles has three columns: from the left, they show the name of the person who sent each message, the size of the message, and the subject of the message. Trumpet arranges messages with the same subject into

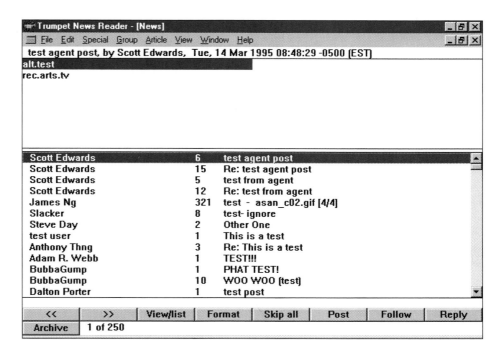

FIGURE 3-5

A list of new messages

thread A series of news articles
on a single subject, organized
with replies immediately following
the original message.

article window In Trumpet
News, the window where the
text of an article appears.

threads, so you can read replies to the original message right after you read
the original.

2. Click the Format button several times to change the way Trumpet displays the list of articles.

3. Double-click on the description of an article to transfer that article to your computer.

When the transfer is complete, the article will appear on your screen, as shown in Figure 3-6. This display is called the **article window.**

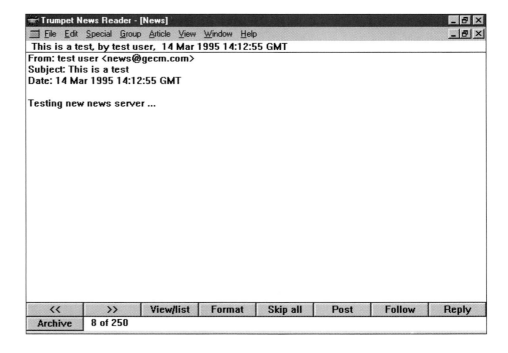

FIGURE 3-6

*A Trumpet News
article window*

4. Click on the View/List button at the bottom of your screen to return to the subject window.

Notice that the description line for the article you just read now has a >> symbol at the left side. This indicates that you have read this article. The next time you request an updated list of articles, Trumpet will only show you the ones you haven't seen before.

The alt.test news group contains test articles from people like you who want to learn how to use Internet news. There are thousands of other news groups out there, and you'll almost certainly find a few that are devoted to subjects that interest you—maybe your favorite television show or type of music, or a hobby, or an area of professional interest.

TRUMPET NEWS BUTTONS

There are nine buttons along the bottom of the Trumpet screen:

<<	The << button displays the article or news group immediately before the current one.
>>	The >> button displays obtains the next article in the current news group, or the next news group.
View/List	Click on the View/List button to switch between the article list and the currently selected article.
Format	When the subject window is visible, clicking the Format button changes the layout of the article list. When the article window is visible, clicking the Format button switches between a proportional type font and a fixed-space font. Figure 3-7 shows an article with a fixed-space font.
	Changing fonts is useful when an article contains a table or a picture constructed from ASCII characters.
Skip All	The Skip All button only works when an article list is visible. Click on the Skip All button to mark all the articles in the current news group as read and move to the next news group.
Post	Use the Post button to send a new article to the current news group. You'll learn more about posting new articles later in this lesson.
Follow	Use the Follow button to write a message in response to the current article.
Reply	Use the Reply button to create a private answer and send it by e-mail to the person who posted the current article. When you send a reply, it does not go to the whole news group.
Archive	Click on the Archive button to save the current article in a folder with the same name as the current news group.

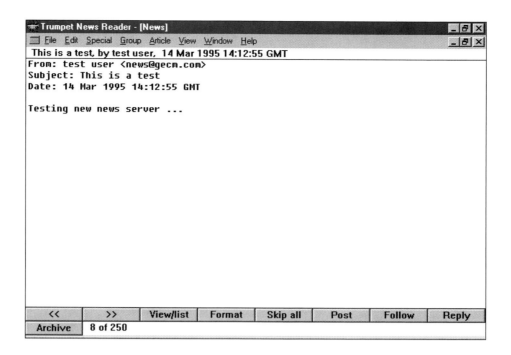

The window shown in the figure contains:

Trumpet News Reader - [News]

File Edit Special Group Article View Window Help

This is a test, by test user, 14 Mar 1995 14:12:55 GMT
From: test user <news@gecm.com>
Subject: This is a test
Date: 14 Mar 1995 14:12:55 GMT

Testing new news server ...

| << | >> | View/list | Format | Skip all | Post | Follow | Reply |
| Archive | 8 of 250 | | | | | | |

FIGURE 3-7

*A news article with
a fixed-space font*

CREATING A NEWS ARTICLE

After you have read the articles in a news group for a while, you may want to become a more active participant. You might have a question about the news group's topic, or you may have some news that you think other subscribers to the news group might want to know about. In this section, you will learn how to create a new article and how to post it to a news group:

HANDS ON

1. If it is not already visible, click the View/List button to display the subject window.

2. Select the **alt.test** news group.

3. Click on the Post button at the bottom of the screen.

   The Post Article window in Figure 3-8 will appear.

4. Press Tab to move the cursor to the **Subject** field.

5. Type a brief description of the article in the Subject field. For this exercise, type **Test Article**

6. Press Tab three times to move the cursor to the **Distribution** field.

7. Type **local** in the Distribution field. This will limit distribution of this article to your local news server.

   To post a message to the whole Internet, you leave the Distribution field empty, but you should specify local distribution for this test article because there's no good reason to send copies to other users all over the world.

8. Press Tab again to move to the body of the article.

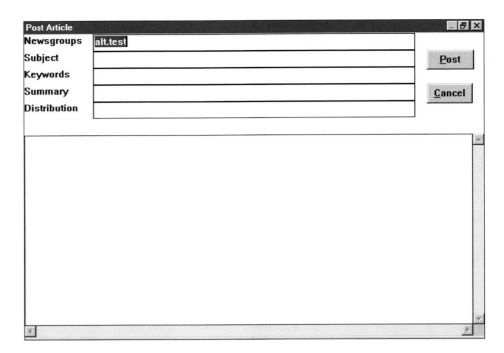

FIGURE 3-8

The Post Article window as it first appears

9. Type this message: **This is a test. Please ignore.**

The content of your article really doesn't matter, because nobody ever reads the messages in alt.test. However, there are a handful of news servers around the world that automatically reply to test messages; the word "ignore" is a signal to those servers to disregard your message.

10. Click on the Post button to transmit your article.

After you send an article to a news group, it may take some time before the news server adds it to the list of unread articles. Don't be alarmed if you don't see it on a message list immediately.

REPLYING TO A NEWS ARTICLE

As you read articles in news groups, you will sometimes want to add your own comments to an ongoing discussion. In some cases, you might have the answer to a question, or you may have some additional information about the original topic.

There are two ways to reply to a news article. You can post it as an article for general distribution, or you can send it as a private e-mail message to the person who posted the original message.

If you post a news article as a reply rather than a new message, many Internet news reader programs will display it as part of a conversation, called a thread, which displays replies immediately following the original message. Trumpet News arranges messages into threads, but it doesn't always show which messages are originals and which are replies.

When you reply to an article, it's a good idea to include a short excerpt from the original; this gives the people reading your answer a better idea what you're talking about. Trumpet News automatically quotes the original message in replies and follow-up articles.

POSTING A FOLLOW-UP ARTICLE

Here's what you need to do to send a reply to the entire news group:

HANDS ON

1. Click on the View/List button to return to the subject window.

2. Select the first article description in the lower half of the subject window.

3. Click on the Follow button at the bottom of the window.

The Post Article window appears, as shown in Figure 3-9.

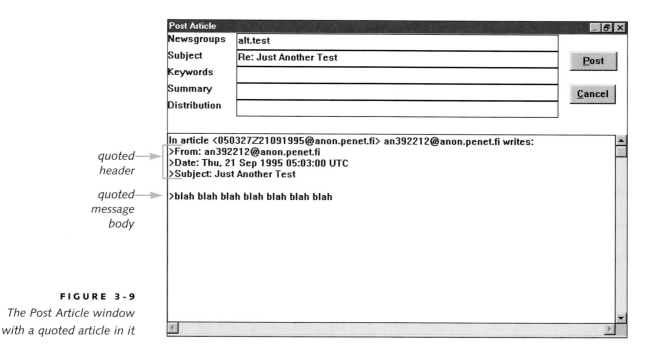

quoted → header

quoted → message body

FIGURE 3-9

The Post Article window with a quoted article in it

Notice that the name of the news group and the subject of the original article are already filled in, and the text of the original article is in the lower portion of the window with a > symbol at the beginning of each line.

4. Press ⌈Tab⌋ four times to move the cursor to the **Distribution** field.

5. Type **local** in the Distribution field to limit distribution of this article to your local server.

NOTE   *When you reply to a real article, leave the Distribution field blank.*

6. Select the quoted header in the lower portion of the window.

7. Press ⌈Delete⌋ to erase the header.

Since the top line of the message body shows the name of the person who sent the original article, there's no need to quote the other information in the header. If the original message is longer than three or four lines, it's a good idea to delete unnecessary portions of the original article. This will make your reply easier to read.

8. Move the cursor to the end of the quoted message and press [Enter] twice. This will add a blank line between the original article and the beginning of your reply.

9. Type your comments, answer, or other reply to the original article, as shown in Figure 3-10.

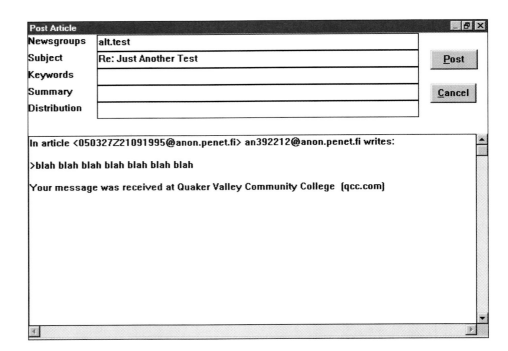

FIGURE 3-10
The Post Article window with a quoted message and a reply

10. Click the Post button to send your article to the news group, including the quotes from the original.

SENDING A REPLY AS E-MAIL

Posting a public message is not always the best way to reply to a news article. For example, if you read one of the hobby news groups, you might find an article that lists collector's items for sale. The sender is the only person you want to reply to, so the best way to send your answer is an e-mail message to the person who sent the original.

HANDS ON

1. Select an article from the subject window.

2. Click on the Reply button at the bottom of the Trumpet window.

The Mail Article window shown in Figure 3-11 will appear. Notice that this window is almost identical to the Post Article window.

Trumpet News has automatically filled in the name and e-mail address of the person who posted the original message and the subject. It has also placed your own name and address in the Cc field, so you will receive a copy of this message via e-mail unless you delete the contents of this field.

3. Place the cursor to the end of the quoted text.

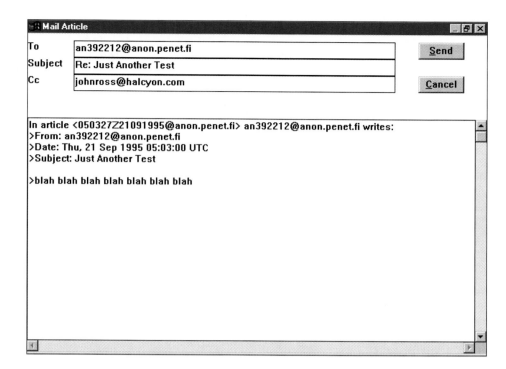

FIGURE 3-11

The reply editor as it first appears

4. Type a sentence or two as a reply to the original message.

5. Since you don't really want to send this message, click on the Cancel button.

If this was a real message, you would click on the Send button instead. When you send a message, Trumpet News displays a Progress window for a few seconds.

6. When the text of the original message appears, double-click on the Trumpet icon in the upper-left corner of the window to close the news reader program.

MAILING LISTS

mailing list An online discussion group that distributes articles by e-mail. When you send a message to the list server, it automatically distributes the message to all of the participants in the mailing list.

In addition to Usenet and the other news groups, there's one other common way that people conduct conferences on the Internet: **mailing lists**. Some mailing lists limit access to members of the sponsoring group, while others are open to anybody who wants to join. The rules of netiquette are exactly the same for mailing lists as for news groups; the only difference is that you send and receive articles by e-mail.

Participants in a mailing list mail their articles to a computer that automatically re-mails them to everybody on the list. Some mailing lists relay new messages as they receive them, while others gather each day's messages into a "digest," and send them as one big message.

Mailing list descriptions usually contain detailed instructions for joining. In general, to get information about a mailing list, you must send a request to the list keeper that includes your own e-mail address and some kind of key word, such as "join" or "subscribe."

LESSON SUMMARY AND EXERCISES

After completing this lesson, you should know the following:

HOW INTERNET NEWS IS ORGANIZED

- There are thousands of separate news groups.

- Each news group is part of a major category, such as *comp*, *rec*, or *alt*.

CONFIGURING TRUMPET NEWS

- Use the Setup dialog box to specify the location of your news server.

READING NEWS

- To subscribe to a new news group in Trumpet News, select Subscribe in the Group menu and select the news group from the list.

- To see a list of articles in a news group in Trumpet, double-click on the name of the news group.

- To read an article, double-click on the listing for that article.

TRUMPET NEWS BUTTONS

- To move between articles in a news group, use the >> and << buttons.

- To switch between the article list and the current article, click the View/List button.

- To change the appearance of your screen, use the Format button.

- To mark all the articles in a news group as read, click the Skip All button.

- To send an article, use the Post, Follow and Reply buttons.

- To save the current article, click the Archive button.

CREATING A NEWS ARTICLE

- To create a new article in a news group, click on the Post button.

- To create an article that answers an existing article, click on the Follow button.

REPLYING TO A NEWS ARTICLE

- To send a private reply to an article as e-mail, click on the Reply button.

MAILING LISTS

- Mailing lists are discussions distributed via e-mail. To join a mailing list, send a request to the list keeper.

NEW TERMS TO REMEMBER

After completing this lesson, you should know the meaning of these terms:

article	news group
article window	news reader
FAQ	news server
mailing list	subscribe
moderated news group	thread
netiquette	Usenet
news	

MATCHING EXERCISE

Match each of the terms with the definitions on the right:

TERMS	DEFINITIONS
1. Usenet	**a.** A program that downloads news from the Internet and displays articles on a PC or other computer
2. mailing list	**b.** The system that circulates news groups to computers around the world
3. news reader	**c.** A list of "frequently asked questions" about a specific topic
4. thread	**d.** A computer that transfers news between the Internet and individual users
5. netiquette	**e.** To instruct your news reader to regularly check for new articles about a specific topic
6. news server	**f.** A set of articles related to a specific topic
7. subscribe	**g.** The informal rules for participating in news groups
8. news group	**h.** An online conversation in which one user posts an article and other users post responses to the original article
9. FAQ	**i.** A discussion about a particular topic, distributed by e-mail

COMPLETION EXERCISE

Fill in the missing word or phrase for each of the following statements:

1. A set of articles about a single topic is called a _____.

2. Trumpet News uses the _____ dialog to specify the name of your news server.

3. To read articles in a news group, you must _____ to that news group.

4. To move to the next news group in Trumpet News, use the _____ button.

5. To toggle between the list of articles and the currently highlighted article in Trumpet News, use the _____ button.

6. To restrict distribution of a news article to your own news server, specify _____ in the distribution field.

7. A discussion distributed by e-mail is called a _____.

8. Before you post a question to a news group, read the _____.

9. To save a copy of the current article in Trumpet News, use the _____ button.

10. To create an article about a new subject in Trumpet News, click on the _____ button.

SHORT-ANSWER QUESTIONS

Write a brief answer to each of the following questions:

1. Usenet organizes news groups into seven major categories. Name four of them.

2. What does the header of a news article contain?

3. What's a mailing list?

4. How would you add a new news group to your subscription list?

5. In which Usenet news group category would you look for a discussion about Windows?

6. What's the difference between a reply and a follow-up article?

APPLICATION PROJECTS

Perform the following actions to complete these projects:

1. Open the *alt.test* news group and post this message:

This is another test. Please ignore it.

2. Add the *alt.food.chocolate* news group to your subscription list.

3. Display the list of articles in *alt.food.chocolate*.

4. Find the FAQ for *alt.food.chocolate* and open it.

5. Save a copy of the chocolate FAQ to your hard drive.

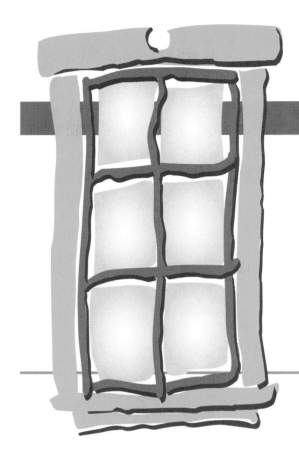

LESSON 4

TELNET AND FTP: OPERATING DISTANT COMPUTERS AND OBTAINING FILES

OBJECTIVES

After completing this lesson, you will be able to do the following:

- *Use the telnet protocol to log in to a remote computer through the Internet.*

- *Use the TN3270 protocol to log in to a remote computer that uses IBM 3270 terminal emulation.*

- *Use FTP (File Transfer Protocol) to copy programs and data files across the Internet from other computers to your PC.*

HOST

Host: host

Port: 23

Language File: English

Ok

n the last two lessons, you learned about methods for exchanging messages through the Internet. E-mail and news are both "store-and-forward" systems that use the Internet as a relatively fast way to move information around. But there are several other things you can do when you connect your computer directly to another computer via the Internet. This lesson tells you how to make your PC into a remote terminal for a second computer, which may be located in the next room, or halfway around the world. It also explains how to use FTP (File Transfer Protocol) to exchange programs, documents and other data files between your own PC and other computers on the Internet.

INTRODUCTION TO TELNET

Telnet is the TCP/IP protocol that connects one computer to a second computer, which treats the first computer like a terminal. When you have a telnet connection, the commands you type on your own computer's keyboard go directly to a distant computer, which is called the telnet host, just as if you were using a terminal attached directly to the host. If you have an account on the remote system, you can use it to run programs, store files, and anything else that you would be able to do on the same machine locally.

When the Internet was first created, its purpose was to allow researchers and scientists to use distant computers without leaving their own offices or laboratories. In those days, a computer with less power than a modern PC was the size of three or four refrigerators, and cost about as much as a suburban house. Therefore, these early Internet users used telnet to access computer resources that were not available locally, and to share their work with people who were hundreds or thousands of miles away.

You may have a powerful computer on your desk, but telnet is still an important Internet tool. It enables you to directly connect to a distant computer, without using long distance telephone lines.

In general, telnet is useful for two kinds of connection:

■ Remote access to a computer where you have an account.

■ Connection to a computer that offers public access, such as a library catalog.

A good telnet program is transparent, like a window that looks through the Internet to a distant host; the real action is on the host. After it makes the connection, you can pay attention to programs running on the host instead of the telnet program.

HOW TELNET WORKS

Compared to other Internet tools, telnet is a relatively simple process: you identify a telnet host, and the telnet program makes the connection. Once you're connected, you must send your login information to the host.

Some telnet hosts display complete instructions for logging in, others ask for your name and passwords, and still others give you a completely blank screen until you press [Enter]. In most cases, if the people who own a telnet host want their system to be easy for visitors to use, they will give it a friendly login like the one in Figure 4-1.

```
Telnet - [iris.unl.edu]                                    _ | B | X
  File   Connect   Window                                  _ | B | X

Welcome to IRIS (Innovative Research Information System)
of the University Libraries and the Law Library of the
University of Nebraska-Lincoln

Public users type "library" (small case) at the login prompt.


login: █
```

FIGURE 4-1
A telnet login message

TERMINAL EMULATION

terminal A device that sends input signals to a computer, usually from a keyboard, and receives output signals from the computer and displays them on a screen or printer.

VT-100 The model number of a computer terminal made by the Digital Equipment Corporation. Since many computers recognize the VT-100's signaling format, it is a standard used by many other terminal makers and terminal emulation programs.

dumb terminal A computer terminal with no built-in processing power.

When most computers were very big and very expensive, users communicated with them through devices called **terminals**. At about the same time that the Internet started, many of the most commonly-used computers were made by the Digital Equipment Corporation (DEC). Digital's model number for the terminal that was used with those computers was the **VT-100**. Since a VT-100 terminal does not have any built-in computing power, it is sometimes known as a **dumb terminal**. Other companies made terminals that used the same signaling format as a VT-100, and other computers also accepted terminals that used the VT-100 format.

When you use a PC to communicate with a second computer, either directly or through the Internet, the PC runs a communications program that imitates a dumb terminal. This is called **terminal emulation**. Both ends of a communication link must use the same kind of terminal emulation. Some communications programs and some host computers offer you a choice of

terminal emulation A computer program that makes the computer's connection to a second computer appear to the second computer as if it was receiving signals from a specific type of terminal. In this way, computers that would otherwise be incompatible can communicate with another.

3270 The model number of a widely-used IBM terminal. Many IBM mainframes require 3270 terminal emulation.

terminal emulation types, while others are limited to just one. Most telnet applications provide VT-100 terminal emulation.

VT-100 terminal emulation is the most common type for almost all hosts on the Internet, except for some IBM mainframe computers, which use a terminal emulation called **3270**. Like the Digital VT-100, 3270 was the model number of the original IBM terminal that used this format. You won't see hosts that expect 3270 emulation as often as those that use VT-100, but when you need to connect to a 3270 host, you will need a special kind of telnet program called TN3270. If you try to connect to a 3270 host with a VT-100 terminal emulator, the host may refuse to accept the connection.

MAKING A TELNET CONNECTION

Trumpet Telnet is a telnet application for Windows. When you become familiar with Trumpet Telnet, you will also know enough to use most other telnet programs.

In this section, you will start the program and set up a telnet connection.

If your PC is running Windows 95, follow these steps to start Trumpet Telnet:

HANDS ON

1. Click the Start button to open the Startup menu, and click on **Programs** to open the Program menu.

2. Choose **Internet Tools** from the Program menu.

3. Choose **Trumpet Telnet** from the Internet Tools menu.

If your PC is using Windows 3.1, follow these steps to start Trumpet Telnet:

HANDS ON

1. Double-click on the Internet Tools icon in the Windows Desktop to open the Internet Tools program group.

2. Double-click on the Trumpet Telnet icon.

When you start Trumpet Telnet, the Host dialog box, as shown in Figure 4-2, asks for the address of a telnet host.

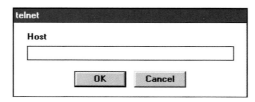

FIGURE 4-2
The telnet Host dialog box

Next you'll connect via telnet to the Spacelink bulletin board operated by the National Aeronautics and Space Administration (NASA).

3. Type **spacelink.msfc.nasa.gov** in the Host dialog box and click the OK button.

Trumpet Telnet will connect you to the Spacelink bulletin board operated by the National Aeronautics and Space Administration (NASA). Figure 4-3 shows Trumpet Telnet connected to Spacelink.

FIGURE 4-3
The Spacelink welcome screen

Notice that the login message tells you that you must emulate a VT-100 terminal. Trumpet Telnet automatically provides VT-100 emulation.

4. Type **guest** at the login prompt.

5. When the welcome screen appears, press Enter.

If you're curious about NASA's space flight activities, you can follow the instructions on your screen to display a menu of information bulletins.

BREAKING THE CONNECTION

When you log off the distant host system, the host normally breaks the telnet connection. This is similar to hanging up a telephone to break the connection.

HANDS ON

1. To break the connection from Spacelink, type **q** for quit, and **y** for yes.

After the connection ends, Trumpet Telnet will automatically close.

MAKING A TN3270 CONNECTION

IBM 3270 terminal emulation uses a somewhat different set of signals, and it uses some function keys that are not included in VT-100 emulation, so it requires a different telnet program. QWS3270 is a TN3270 telnet program for Windows.

If you are using Windows 95, follow this procedure to start QWS3270:

HANDS ON

1. Click the Start button to open the Startup menu, and click on **Programs** to open the Program menu.

2. Choose **Internet Tools** from the Program menu.

3. Choose **QWS3270** from the Internet Tools menu.

To start QWS3270 from Windows 3.1, double-click on the QWS3270 icon in the Program Manager's Internet Tools program group.

The Texas A&M University Statewide Network is a telnet host that requires 3270 terminal emulation. Follow these steps to connect to the Texas network:

HANDS ON

1. When the Winsock 3270 telnet screen appears, choose the **Connect** command from the menu bar.

The Host dialog box, in Figure 4-4 will appear.

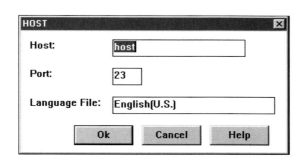

FIGURE 4-4
The QWS3270 Host dialog box

2. Type **TAMMVS1.TAMU.EDU** in the **Host** field and click the OK button.

QWS3270 will connect your computer to the Texas A&M University Statewide Network. When the connection is established, your screen will display a welcoming screen like the one in Figure 4-5.

FIGURE 4-5
The welcome screen from
Texas A&M University

Notice that a row of buttons has appeared at the bottom of the QWS3270 window. These buttons correspond to some of the special function keys on an IBM 3270 terminal.

3. Choose the **Options** command from the Setup menu to display the dialog box in Figure 4-6.

FIGURE 4-6
The QWS3270 Options
Setup dialog box

4. Click the box next to Button Bars: **Line 2**.

There should be check marks in both Button Bars' Yes/No boxes.

5. Click the OK button to close the dialog box.

Notice that there are now two rows of on-screen buttons across the bottom of the QWS3270 window.

6. Since you don't really want to use the computer in Texas, break the connection by clicking on the Close command in the menu bar.

QWS3270 will break the connection and close the program window. When you actually log in to a remote 3270 host, the host will break the connection after you log off.

DOWNLOADING FILES WITH FTP

Telnet allows you to connect your own computer to others across the Internet, but the Internet also contains many collections of software and data files that you may want to use on your own PC. In order to move files between computers, you must use a tool called File Transfer Protocol, better known as FTP.

If you have an account on the distant computer that contains the files you want to copy, it's a simple matter to send that computer your login name and password. But there are also hundreds of collections of software and data files that are available to anybody who wants to use them. These may include articles from popular magazines and scholarly journals, satellite weather maps, recipes, software for your PC, and a huge variety of other material. The standard method for connecting to an FTP archive where you don't have an account is called **anonymous FTP**.

anonymous FTP The process of logging in to an FTP server where you don't have an account with the account name "anonymous" and your e-mail address as password.

HOW FTP WORKS

In this lesson, you will use an FTP program for Windows that makes moving files across the Internet relatively easy. But since you may encounter other FTP programs on other computers, you really should understand what's happening underneath the graphic screen.

There are four steps to an FTP file transfer:

■ Log in to the FTP Server. The most common type of FTP file transfer is anonymous FTP from a public archive. To log in to an anonymous FTP site, you must use the word *anonymous* as your login name, and your own e-mail address as your password.

If you have an account on a distant computer, you can use the same login name for both telnet and FTP.

■ Find the file you want. Almost every computer on the Internet uses a directory structure similar to the one on your PC, with directories that may contain subdirectories and individual files. Before you can transfer a file, you must either specify the full directory path or move to the directory that contains the file you want to transfer.

The people who maintain anonymous FTP archives sometimes provide some information that will make it easier for you to find the files you want. Sometimes, this information appears automatically when you log in, or when you move to a new directory. But more often, you'll see files called INDEX.TXT, or READ.ME, or possibly README.FIRST or something similar. It's almost always worth the time and trouble to see what these files contain. Most FTP programs have some kind of "view" command that will import a text file from the server and display it on your screen.

■ Download the file. After you find the name of the file you want to transfer, you must tell the server to send you a copy. Of course, it's not that simple. An FTP archive may contain both ASCII documents and binary program files. An ASCII file contains text; a binary file might be a program that runs on your PC, or it could be a program for some other kind of computer. If you know where to look, you can find an archive of programs for just about any computer built in the last thirty years.

Since FTP uses different methods for moving ASCII text files and binary program files, you have to identify the type of file before you transfer it. If you use the wrong kind of file transfer, your computer won't be able to make any sense of the file it receives.

■ Close the connection. After you finish moving files between the FTP server and your PC, you must break the link. An FTP server can handle only a limited number of connections at one time; since many of the most popular FTP archives receive hundreds of requests for downloads every day, it's a courtesy to other Internet users to disconnect as soon as your download is complete.

CONNECTING TO AN ANONYMOUS FTP SERVER

In this section, you will use John Junod's Winsock FTP Client (WS-FTP) to connect to an anonymous FTP server. WS-FTP is a tool for moving text and data files across the Internet to and from your PC. It replaces standard Unix FTP commands with a graphic screen that makes the whole process a great deal easier to manage.

Follow these steps to start WS-FTP in Windows 95:

HANDS ON

1. Click the Start button to open the Startup menu, and click on **Programs** to open the Program menu.

2. Choose **Internet Tools** from the Program menu.

3. Choose **WS-FTP** from the Internet Tools menu.

In Windows 3.1, double-click on the WS-FTP icon in the Internet Tools program group window.

The Session Profile dialog box in Figure 4-7 will appear.

4. Click **New**.

5. Move the cursor to the **Host Name** field and type **ftp.msstate.edu**

6. Click the **Anonymous Login** box.

The word "anonymous" will appear in the User ID field.

7. Move the cursor to the **Password** field, and type your e-mail address.

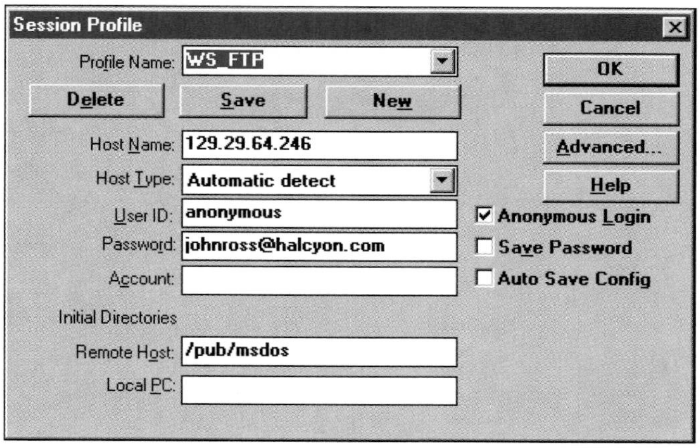

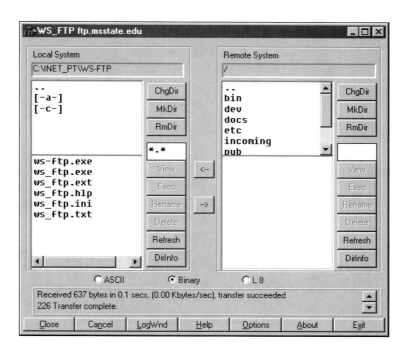

FIGURE 4-7
The WS-FTP Session Profile dialog box

8. Click the OK button.

The Session Profile dialog box will disappear, and Winsock FTP will connect your computer to an FTP archive at Mississippi State University. The main Winsock FTP screen in Figure 4-8 will appear on your screen.

FIGURE 4-8
The main Winsock FTP screen

The main Winsock FTP screen displays two directories: your own PC's directory is on the left and the directory of the remote system that you're currently connected to is on the right. The upper box in each directory shows subdirectories under the current directory, and the lower section shows files in the current directory. To the right of each directory are nine buttons:

■ ChgDir (Change Directory). To move to a different directory, select the subdirectory you want to move to and click the ChgDir button. Choose .. to move up one level.

- MkDir (Make Directory). Click on the MkDir button to create a new subdirectory under the current directory. This button does not work on the remote system when you're connected via anonymous FTP.

- RmDir (Remove Directory). To delete a subdirectory, select its name and click the RmDir button. This button does not work on the remote system when you're connected via anonymous FTP.

- View. To display the contents of a text file or a data file, select the name of the file and click the View button.

- Exec (Execute). To run a program, select its name and click the Exec button. If you Click on the Exec button for the Remote System, Winsock FTP will transfer the program to your PC before it runs the program.

- Rename. Highlight the name of a file and click on the Rename button to change the name of the file. This button does not work on remote files when you're on an anonymous connection.

- Delete. To remove a file from the current directory, select the name of that file and click the Delete button. This button does not work on remote files when you're on an anonymous connection.

- Refresh. Click the Refresh button to display a new (and updated) version of the current directory.

- DirInfo (Directory Information). Click on the DirInfo button to display details about the current directory; this will usually include the size and creation date of each file and subdirectory.

FINDING A FILE

Once you're connected to an FTP server, your next step is to locate the file you want to download. For example, Mississippi State University has an FTP archive of historical documents, including the text of Lincoln's Gettysburg Address. Here's how to locate that file:

HANDS ON

1. Move the scroll bar at the left of the remote directory box, until you see the listing for the **pub** directory.

Like many other FTP archives, the one at Mississippi State has placed files that they hope you will want to download in a directory called **pub** (short for public).

2. Select the **pub** directory and click on the ChgDir button.

After a short wait, you will see a list of topics in the remote directory box. Each topic is a subdirectory containing files related to that topic.

3. Select **docs** in the directory list and click on the ChgDir button.

4. As new lists of directories appear in the directory list, choose **history**, and then **USA**, and finally **19th_C**.

The list of historical documents in Figure 4-9 will appear in the remote file list.

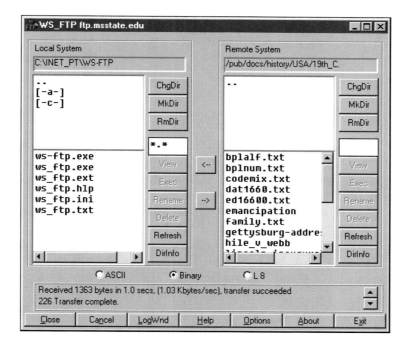

FIGURE 4-9

The Winsock screen with the 19th Century Historical Documents directory

VIEWING A TEXT FILE

After you locate a file, you may want to take a look at it before you store a copy on your hard drive. Here's how to do it:

HANDS ON

1. Select the file **gettysburg-address**.

2. Click on the View button.

A Transfer Status window will appear while Winsock FTP obtains the file from the server. When the transfer is complete, Winsock FTP will load the text into the Notepad text editor, as shown in Figure 4-10.

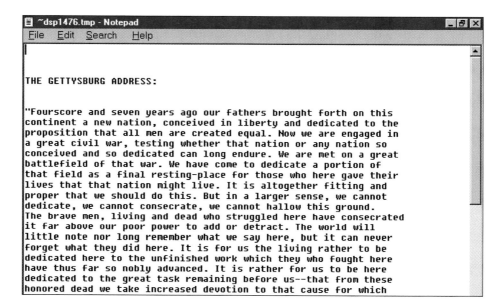

FIGURE 4-10

The Gettysburg Address document imported from Mississippi State

If you want to print a copy of the text file, or save a copy on your hard drive, you can use the commands in the text editor. After you're finished reading the text file (and saving it if you wish), you're ready to close the text editor.

3. Select **Exit** from the File menu to close the text editor.

4. Click on the Close button in the lower-left corner of the Winsock FTP screen to break the connection to Mississippi State.

DOWNLOADING A FILE

The View command is convenient when you want to see the contents of a text file before you save it, but often you will want to download and save a file without reading it first. And since many files contain compressed data, you will need to download them before you can expand and use the programs in those files.

In this section, you will connect to another FTP archive and download the Declaration of Independence from an archive at the University of Washington in Seattle.

1. Click on the Connect button at the lower-left corner of the Winsock FTP window.

The Session Profile dialog box will appear.

2. Click on the New button to clear the connection profile fields.

3. Move your cursor to the **Host Name** field.

4. Type **ftp.uwtc.washington.edu**

5. Click on the box next to Anonymous Login to fill in the **User ID** and **Password** fields.

6. Click on the OK button.

Winsock FTP will connect you to the server at **uwtc.washington.edu**.

7. Double-click on the **pub** directory in the upper-right window.

8. Double-click on the **docs** directory.

9. Double-click on the **HistoricalDocs** directory listing to display the directory in Figure 4-11.

10. Since the file you want to transfer is an ASCII text file, click on the **ASCII** radio button under the directory windows. It's a safe bet that any file with a *.txt* file extension is a text file.

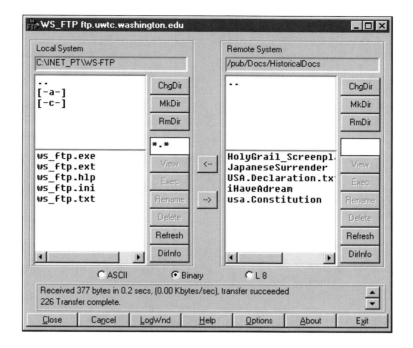

FIGURE 4-11

The University of Washington's HistoricalDocs directory

When you transfer a program file, including those with *.zip* and *.exe* file extensions, use the **Binary** radio button. Use the **L8** radio button when you transfer program files from a computer that uses the VMS operating system. You probably won't see L8 files very often.

11. Select the **USA.Declaration.txt** file.

12. Click the **<–** button.

Winsock FTP will transfer a copy of the text file to your PC.

13. Click on the Close button at the bottom-right corner of the Winsock FTP window.

If you want to read the Declaration, highlight the new **USA.dec** file in the Local System directory and click on the View button.

ENDING AN FTP SESSION

Follow these steps to shut down the Winsock FTP program:

HANDS ON

1. If you haven't already broken the connection to the FTP server, click the Close button.

2. Click on the Exit button in the lower-right corner of the window.

EXPANDING COMPRESSED FILES

Many files in FTP archives have been compressed in order to save space on the host computer's disk drive, and reduce the amount of time needed to download them. In order to use a compressed file after you download it, you must restore the file to its original size with an expansion program.

The most common compression format for DOS and Windows files uses the file extension *.zip*. To restore a .zip file to its original size, use a program such as *PKUNZIP*, which is available via anonymous FTP from the archive at *pkware.com*, in the directory */pub/pkware*. When you connect to the *pkware* archive, read the text file called *"files"* to find the name of the file that contains the current version of *PKUNZIP*. When this was written, the program was in a file called *pkz204.exe*. This is a self-extracting file, so you won't need *PKUNZIP* to open it. Remember to set WS-FTP to "binary" before you transfer the file.

After you have downloaded and installed *pkunzip*, use the Options command in the Windows 95 View menu to associate the .ZIP file extension with *PKUNZIP.EXE*. If you're using Windows 3.X, use the Associate command in the File Manager's File menu.

While .zip files are the most common in PC applications, there are many others that you might occasionally see. You can obtain a large list of formats and sources for programs to uncompress them in a file called *"compression,"* which is available via anonymous FTP from *ftp.cso.uiuc.edu*, in the directory *doc/pcnet*.

FINDING FTP ARCHIVES

The disk that accompanies this book contains a list of almost a thousand anonymous FTP sites in all parts of the world. These archives have thousands of data files and programs that you may download and use. The list is in two forms: *textlist.exe* contains a self-extracting text file, and *ftp-list.exe* contains the same information in a set of HyperText Markup Language (HTML) files that you can use with a web browser application program such as Microsoft's Internet Explorer or Netscape Navigator. You will learn how to use web browsers in Lesson 6.

Please note that new FTP archives appear and old ones disappear all the time. The lists on the disk were up-to-date when they were created, but you may not be able to reach all of the archives. You can find instructions for obtaining a more recent version of the list in the *READ-ME.TXT* file on the disk.

Follow these steps to use the lists on the disk:

HANDS ON

1. Create a new directory on your hard drive.

2. Copy the file you want to use to the new directory.

3. Use the **Run** command in the Windows 3.1 File Manager or the Windows 95 Start menu to run the program you just copied to your hard drive.

4. Use a text editor or word processor such as Write or WordPad to read the text files, or a web browser such as Microsoft's Internet Explorer or Netscape Navigator to view the .html files.

LESSON SUMMARY AND EXERCISES

After completing this lesson, you should know how to do the following:

INTRODUCTION TO TELNET

■ To connect your computer to another computer as a terminal, use the telnet protocol.

HOW TELNET WORKS

■ To log in to a remote host that expects VT-100 terminal emulation, use a telnet client program, such as Trumpet Telnet.

■ To log in to a remote host that expects IBM 3270 terminal emulation, use a TN3270 program, such as QWS3270.

■ To identify the distant computer to which you want to connect, use the Internet address of that host.

MAKING A TELNET CONNECTION

■ To set up a telnet connection with Trumpet Telnet, type the name of the computer to which you want to connect in the Host dialog box.

■ To start using the distant computer after you connect, type the information requested by the distant system.

■ To break a connection, log off the distant system.

MAKING A TN3270 CONNECTION

■ To connect to an IBM mainframe, use 3270 terminal emulation.

■ To use QWS3270, select the Connect command from the menu bar and type the address of the host system.

DOWNLOADING FILES WITH FTP

■ To use File Transfer Protocol (FTP) for downloading files from other computers on the Internet, use an FTP client program such as WS-FTP.

CONNECTING TO AN ANONYMOUS FTP SERVER

■ For anonymous connection to an FTP host, use "anonymous" as your login name, and your e-mail address as password.

■ To transfer a file, move through the host's directory structure until you find the file you want.

■ In WS-FTP, highlight a file name and click the <– to download a copy of that file to your PC.

EXPANDING COMPRESSED FILES

■ To expand compressed files, use a program such as *PKUNZIP*.

FINDING FTP ARCHIVES

■ The disk that accompanies this book contains a large list of FTP archives.

NEW TERMS TO REMEMBER

After completing this lesson, you should know the meaning of these terms:

3270	terminal
anonymous FTP	terminal emulation
dumb terminal	VT-100

MATCHING EXERCISE

Match each of the terms with the definitions on the right:

TERMS	DEFINITIONS
1. FTP	**a.** A terminal with no built-in computing power
2. telnet	**b.** The model number of a Digital Equipment Corporation terminal that was widely used in the early days of the Internet
3. dumb terminal	**c.** The process of sending signals to a host computer that appear to be coming from a specific model of terminal
4. VT-100	
5. terminal emulation	**d.** The technique used for transferring files across the Internet
6. 3270 terminal	**e.** The method used for connecting to an FTP archive where the user does not have an account
7. anonymous FTP	
	f. The type of terminal emulation required by many IBM mainframe computers
	g. The protocol that connects one computer through the Internet to a second computer as a terminal

---

COMPLETION EXERCISE

Fill in the missing word or phrase for each of the following statements:

1. The most common type of terminal emulation is called _____.

2. When you connect to an IBM mainframe computer, you may need to use _____ emulation.

3. The Internet tool for remotely connecting to a distant computer is called _____.

4. To set up a telnet connection, type the host's _____ in the Host dialog box.

5. The Internet tool for moving files from one computer to another is called _____, or FTP.

6. To set up an FTP connection to an anonymous FTP archive, use "anonymous" as your login name, and _____ as your password.

7. To move to a different directory on an FTP host, highlight the name of the subdirectory and click on the _____ button.

8. When you transfer a program file via FTP, you must specify a _____ transfer.

9. To download a file from an FTP archive using WS-FTP, highlight the name of the file and click on the _____ button.

10. The most common compression method for Windows and DOS files uses the _____ file extension.

SHORT-ANSWER QUESTIONS

Write a brief answer to each of the following questions:

1. Name two uses for telnet connections.

2. What kind of terminal emulation do IBM mainframes expect?

3. How do you log in to an anonymous FTP site?

4. What are lists of common questions on a particular topic called?

5. In Winsock FTP, how would you move to a different subdirectory?

6. Which Winsock FTP command would you use to display the contents of a text file?

APPLICATION PROJECTS

Perform the following actions to complete these projects:

1. The library catalog at the University of California is called MELVYL. The Internet address is *melvyl.ucop.edu*. Use telnet to connect to MELVYL as a VT-100 terminal. When your connection is in place, use the command "find the wholesale price structure for oranges" to find the name of the author of *The Wholesale Price Structure for Oranges, With Special Reference to the Chicago Auction Market*.

   After you have obtained the author's name, use the Exit command to close the connection.

2. Download a copy of the list of records by the English folksinger Ewan MacColl from the archive at *ftp.halcyon.com* in the directory */local/johnross/discography*.

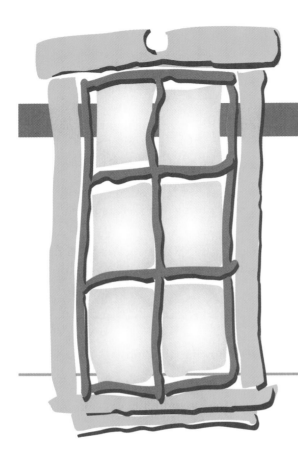

LESSON 5

THE INTERNET GOPHER

OBJECTIVES

*After completing this lesson, you will be able to do the
following:*

- *Understand how the Internet Gopher works.*

- *Navigate through Gopher menus.*

- *Use the WS Gopher program.*

- *Find Internet resources by navigating through
 Gopherspace.*

n the last three lessons, you learned about the different methods that people use to move information across the Internet, including mail, news, telnet, and FTP. There are millions of useful and entertaining items available on the Internet, but unless you know what you're looking for, finding any particular item can be extremely difficult. In this lesson and the next, you will learn about tools that can guide you through the Internet to individual files, data bases, and other resources.

ABOUT GOPHER

Gopher A system of linked menus with pointers to Internet resources and other menus. When a user selects an item from a menu, the Gopher client downloads a copy of the file or menu identified by that menu item.

The Internet **Gopher** is a system of menus that contain pointers to programs, data files, telnet hosts, news groups, and other Gopher Menus. Some Gopher menus are organized by topic, and others are geographical. Therefore, you can use Gopher to find a file or service when you know its approximate location (such as "Kansas" or "Hong Kong"), or you can search through Gopher menus to find material on related topics (such as "weather maps" or "history") that might be located on computers anywhere in the world. You can start at almost any Gopher menu and make your way to any other menu with just a few mouse clicks.

The original Internet Gopher was created at the University of Minnesota (home of the Golden Gophers) to allow users to find information stored on many different on-campus computers. When a user selected an item from a menu, they would see either another menu or the name of a specific file which might be stored on the same computer as the menu or any other computer connected to it through the Internet.

Over time, the number of Gopher menus increased, and the menu listings extended beyond the Minnesota campus to other computers throughout the Internet. Today, there are thousands of Gopher servers all over the world. That portion of the Internet organized into Gopher menus is sometimes called **Gopherspace**.

Gopherspace That portion of the Internet that is accessible through Gopher menus.

NAVIGATING THROUGH GOPHERSPACE

Gopher client A computer program that connects to Gopher servers, displays Gopher menus, and downloads resources listed in those menus.

Gopher server A computer that contains one or more Gopher menus.

In order to use Gopher to search for things on the Internet, you must use a program called a **Gopher client**, which obtains information from the thousands of **Gopher servers**. In this lesson, you will use a Gopher client program for Windows called WS Gopher, but there are many other similar programs. Almost all of them use similar graphical menus, bookmarks, and other features, so you should be able to figure out how to navigate through the Internet with any of them after you work your way through this chapter.

STARTING WS GOPHER

Before you can start searching through Gopherspace, you must start the WS Gopher client program.

Follow these steps if you're using Windows 95:

HANDS ON

1. Click on the Start button to open the Startup menu.

2. Click on **Programs** to open the Program menu.

3. Select **Internet Tools** from the Program menu.

4. Select **WS Gopher** from the Internet Tools menu.

If your PC is running Windows 3.1, use this procedure to start WS Gopher:

HANDS ON

1. Double-click on the Internet Tools icon in the Windows Desktop to open the Internet Tools program group.

2. Double-click on the WS Gopher icon.

WS Gopher uses the top-level Gopher menu at the University of Illinois as its default starting point. The Illinois Gopher has pointers to many other Gopher servers around the world. Figure 5-1 shows the main Illinois Gopher menu screen.

CHANGING FONTS

The default directory font is Courier, which is not as easy to read as some others. It's not difficult to change fonts:

HANDS ON

1. Choose the **Fonts** command from the Configure menu.

The Fonts sub-menu will appear.

2. Choose the **Directory Window** command to display the menu in Figure 5-2.

3. Choose the screen font you want to use from the **Font, Font Style**, and **Size** fields.

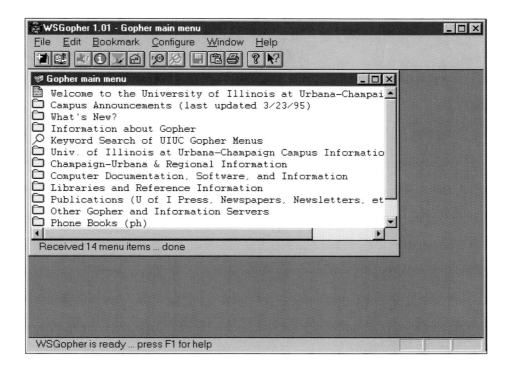

FIGURE 5-1

The main University of Illinois Gopher menu

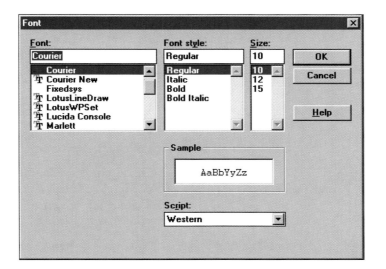

FIGURE 5-2

The WS Gopher Font dialog box

10 point Arial Bold or MS Sans Serif Bold are good choices for Gopher menus. The Sample box shows you what the type font you select will look like on your screen.

4. Click the OK button to save your choice and close the dialog box.

The menu window now looks like Figure 5-3.

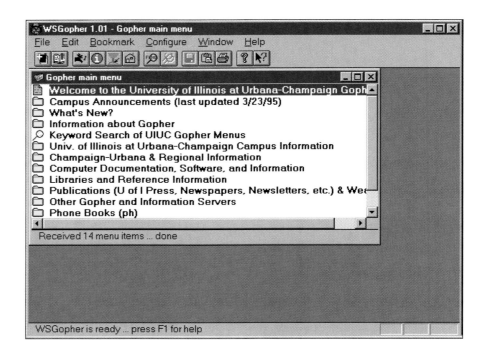

FIGURE 5-3

The Illinois Gopher using the MS Sans Serif font

MOVING AROUND A GOPHER DIRECTORY

Each item in a Gopher menu has an icon to the left of its name. The icon identifies the type of item:

📁	Directory	This item is a jump to another Gopher menu.
📄	Text File	This item is a document.
📞	Phone Book	This item is a jump to an interactive telephone directory. Most telephone directories are located on college or university campuses or businesses.
BH	Bin Hex File	This item is a program file encoded in the Bin Hex format that converts it from binary data to ASCII characters. It is probably a program that will only run on a Macintosh computer.
DOS	DOS Archive	This item is an MS-DOS binary program file.
UU	UUencoded File	This item is a program file encoded in the UUencode format that converts binary data to ASCII characters. It is probably a program for computers that use the Unix operating system.
🔍	Index Search	This item is a database that you can use to search for specific information.
TEL	Telnet Login	This item uses your telnet client program to log you into a remote computer. Before it connects to the host, you may see an information window that tells you how to log in.

	3270 Telnet	This item is a TN3270 telnet connection to a remote computer that requires IBM 3270 terminal emulation. Before it connects to the host, you may see an information window that tells you how to log in.
	Generic Binary File	This item is a binary program file, but WS Gopher is unable to identify the type.
	Image File	This item is a still picture.
	Video File	This item is a moving picture. It might be an animation or a digitized video or movie. Video files are usually very large, so they generally take a long time to download and occupy a lot of space on your hard drive.
	Sound File	This item is an audio recording. Audio files are not as big as videos, but they still may take quite a while to download.
	MIME File	This item is a file encoded in MIME (Multipurpose Internet Mail Extensions) format. MIME is mainly used for e-mail, so you won't see this kind of item very often.
	HTML Page	This item is a World Wide Web page, in Hypertext Markup Language format. You will learn more about the World Wide Web in the next chapter.
	Information	This item is a string of text that the creator of this menu has included to explain something about the current menu. There is no file or jump associated with this item. Some Information items extend beyond a single line. When that happens, you will see an Information icon at the left of each line of text.
	Ask Form	This item is an interactive dialog box that requests additional information, such as a password, your name and address, a switch, or a set of radio buttons.
	Error	This icon appears when the server returns an error message back to WS Gopher. The message may tell you that it is unable to find or connect to the item you requested, or that a server is too busy to accept your request.
	Unknown Item Type	This icon appears when WS Gopher does not recognize the item type.

You probably won't ever see a single menu with all of these item types in it.

When you select an item from a menu, WS Gopher automatically transfers a copy of that item to your PC. If the item is a data file, WS Gopher loads the file into an application program that can display the contents of the file:

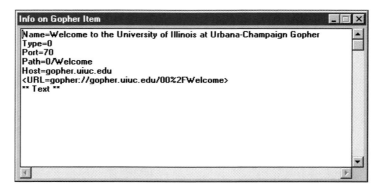

HANDS ON

1. Highlight the first item on the Illinois Gopher main menu, **Welcome to the University of Illinois at Urbana-Champaign Gopher.**

2. Choose the **Info On Item** command from the File menu.

   The information window in Figure 5-4 appears.

FIGURE 5-4

An Item Information window

The information window shows additional details about the currently highlighted item, including the name of the host where this item is located, the full file name, and the item type.

3. Click on the X in the upper-right corner of the information window to close it.

4. Double-click on the **Welcome to the University...** menu item.

   Since this is a text file, WS Gopher will open the file and display it on your screen. Figure 5-5 shows the Welcome text file display.

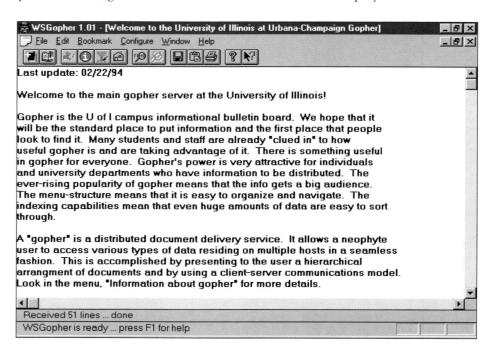

FIGURE 5-5

The Welcome to the University of Illinois text file display

5. Double-click the title bar to expand the window.

6. After you finish reading the Welcome text file, choose the Home Gopher command from the File menu.

The Gopher main menu will return to your screen.

JUMPING TO A DIRECTORY

When you choose a directory from a Gopher menu, you will move to that directory, where you will be able to select additional items, or jump to still another menu.

In this exercise, you will make a series of jumps from the main Gopher server at the University of Illinois to an archive of weather information.

HANDS ON

1. Double-click on the **Other Gopher and Information Servers** item about three-quarters down the menu.

2. When the **Other Gopher...** menu appears, double-click on **The UofI Weather Machine**.

3. When the menu in Figure 5-6 appears, double-click on **States**, near the bottom of the menu. If you get a "busy" message, wait a few minutes and try again.

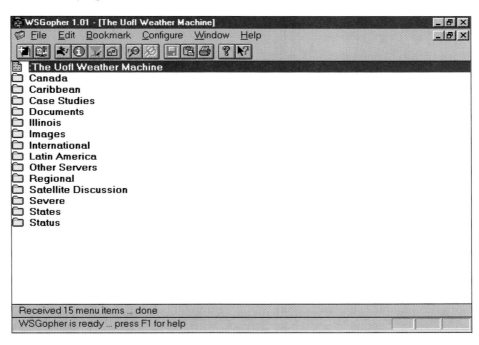

FIGURE 5-6

The UofI Weather Machine menu

After a few seconds, a menu of states will appear.

4. Choose the menu item with the name of your state and double-click on it.

A menu will appear with a list of forecasts and other reports for various cities in your state.

5. Choose the **Metro Area Zone Fcst (forecast)** for the metropolitan area closest to you, or if you're not near a metropolitan area, choose **State Forecast.**

A current weather forecast for your area similar to the one in Figure 5-7 will appear as a text file.

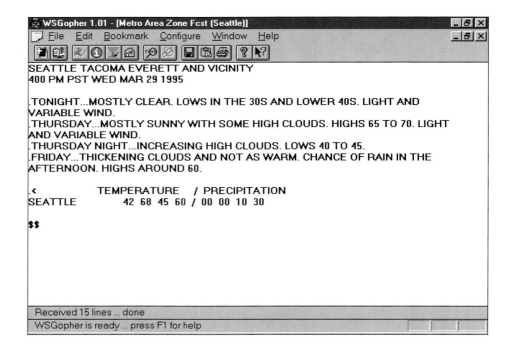

6. After you read the weather forecast, choose the **Cascade** command from the Window menu to display multiple menus within the Gopher window.

BROWSING THROUGH GOPHERSPACE

You can use Gopher to move quickly to a specific item as you did when you found your local weather forecast, but it's often useful to browse around without that much direction, searching for interesting topics, or looking around for items related to a specific topic.

In this exercise, you will learn how to move to other Gopher servers with pointers to every Gopher server in the world, organized by location.

HANDS ON

1. Find the title bar for the **Other Gopher and Information Servers** Gopher menu and click on it.

2. Scroll down to the bottom of the list and double-click on the **USA** directory.

3. When the list of states appears, double-click on **Connecticut.**

A list of all the Gopher servers in the state of Connecticut will appear. You can then jump to any of these servers by double-clicking on a directory item.

OTHER WAYS TO MOVE THROUGH GOPHERSPACE

A geographical search can be pretty efficient when you have a rough idea what you're looking for, but a lot of the time, you won't know the location of the information you want. You can also search Gopherspace by searching through topics.

**HANDS
ON**

1. Go back to the **Other Gopher and Information Servers** menu.

2. Scroll down to the **Recommended Gopher Servers for Exploration** item and double-click on it.

   The menu in Figure 5-8 will appear.

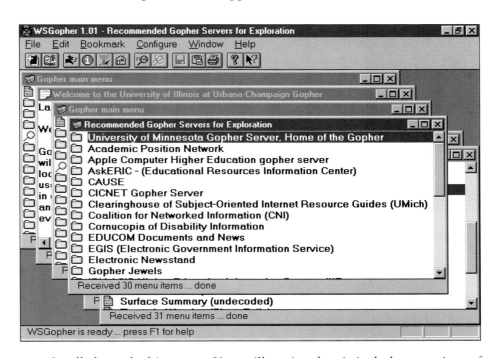

FIGURE 5-8

*The Recommended
Gopher Servers menu*

Scroll through this menu. You will notice that it includes a variety of subject directories, ranging from the Library of Congress to MTV to the National Institute of Allergy and Infectious Disease. Each of these items points to another set of menus that list items related to that topic.

3. Double-click on the **Gopher Jewels** item.

   You will jump to still another list of directories, organized by topic.

4. At this stage, you're on your own for a while. If you see a directory item that looks like an interesting topic, go ahead and select it by double-clicking on it, and follow a few threads to see where they lead. The best way to learn about Gopherspace is to wander around at random.

5. When you're ready to tear yourself away from the strange and wonderful things you've found (or when your instructor tells you to quit), close all of the Gopher windows that are open within the main program window.

JUMPING TO A SPECIFIC GOPHER

Browsing through Gopherspace is one way to find Internet resources, but you can also use a Gopher client program to move directly to a specific menu or a specific item within a menu. This can save you a lot of time.

In this exercise, you will jump directly to the United States Senate's Gopher menu. Follow these steps to move directly to a Gopher menu:

HANDS ON

1. Open the File menu and choose the **New Gopher** command.

The dialog box in Figure 5-9 will appear.

FIGURE 5-9
The new Gopher dialog box

Fetch this Gopher Item		☒
Title:	U.S. Senate Gopher	Paste
Server name:	gopher.senate.gov	
Server port:	70	Ok
Selector:		Cancel
Item type:	Directory ▼ ☐ Gopher Plus	Help
URL:		

2. Type **U.S. Senate Gopher** in the **Title** field.

3. Tab to the **Server Name** field and type **gopher.senate.gov**

4. Click OK.

WS Gopher will retrieve the Senate Gopher menu and display it in a new window.

DEFINING A BOOKMARK

If you find a particularly interesting item in your exploration through Gopherspace, it's a good idea to keep a record of its location, so you can return to the same place later. The easiest way to do this is to create a bookmark that will take you directly back to that item.

In this exercise, you will open an existing bookmark and create a new bookmark for the U. S. Senate Gopher.

HANDS ON

1. Choose **Edit Bookmark** in the Bookmark menu.

2. Scroll down to the bottom of the categories list and double-click the **U.S. Government Information** item.

3. Choose **United States GOVERNMENT Gophers** from the menu.

4. Click the Fetch button.

5. Click OK to close the Bookmark window.

6. Scroll down to the bottom of the Government Gophers menu and click once on **U.S. Senate Gopher**.

7. Choose **Add Bookmark** in the Bookmark menu.

8. Scroll down to the **U.S. Government Information** category and high-light it.

9. Click OK.

You can assign any item to any category. In general, you should choose a category that reminds you of the item for which you are creating a bookmark.

CHANGING YOUR HOME GOPHER

Home Gopher The Gopher menu that a Gopher client program uses as a starting point.

Your **Home Gopher** is the menu that your Gopher client program displays when you first start the program. In general, your Home Gopher should be a menu that can get you to a variety of other high-level menus in one or two jumps. WS Gopher's default Home Gopher, the University of Illinois' main menu is a good choice, but if you find another one you like better, or if your own network or Internet service provider maintains a local Gopher server, it's easy to change.

HANDS ON

1. Open the Configure menu and choose the **Home Gopher Server** command.

The Home Gopher Server(s) dialog box in Figure 5-10 appears.

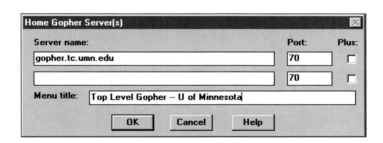

FIGURE 5-10

The Home Gopher Server(s) dialog box

2. When the Home Gopher Server(s) dialog box in Figure 5-10 appears, type **gopher.tc.umn.edu** in the **Server Name** field. This is the top-level Gopher server at the University of Minnesota, which lists every other Gopher server in the world.

The dialog box gives you space for two separate servers. If the first one is busy when you try to connect to it, WS Gopher will try the second server.

3. Type **Top Level Gopher--U of Minnesota** in the **Menu Title** field.

4. Click the OK button.

5. Open the File menu and choose the **Home Gopher** command.

A new menu window will open with the Minnesota Gopher menu in it.

MORE AND BETTER INFORMATION WITH GOPHER+

Most items in Gopher menus are very brief descriptions of a file or menu. But as more and more kinds of items appeared on Gopher menus, it became clear that users would find them easier to use if they had more information than just a one-line description. In 1993, the people responsible for the Gopher standard created an improved version called Gopher Plus (also described in print as Gopher+).

Gopher+ An extended Gopher service that includes additional information about items in Gopher menus.

extended information The information supplied by Gopher+.

Ask Form A dialog box that requests information from the user.

Gopher+ adds two kinds of features to the original version of Gopher (sometimes called "Gopher plain"). Each Gopher+ item listing provides **extended information** about that item, including a more detailed description of the item, detailed administrative information, and when appropriate, a list of alternative versions of the same file. Alternate versions might offer the same text file in more than one language, or in formats for more than one type of word processor. A graphic file might offer alternate views in several different file formats.

The second important feature of Gopher+ is an interactive item called an **Ask Form**. An Ask Form is a menu item that opens a dialog box that can include text fields, switches, and menus of files. The administrator of a Gopher server can use an Ask Form to obtain detailed information from the user before sending a file.

WS Gopher is compatible with both Gopher and Gopher+. The menus look the same, but when you connect to a Gopher+ server, you can obtain additional information about the items in each menu by using the Info On Item command in the File menu.

SEARCHING FOR GOPHER RESOURCES

There are thousands of Gopher servers, with more than fifteen million separate items in their menus. Short of spending hours and hours stepping through menus, how do you find a particular item, or all available items on a particular subject? **Veronica** (Very Easy Rodent-Oriented Net-wide Index to Computerized Archives—and yes, there are other search tools called Archie and Jughead) is a keyword search tool that finds information items in existing Gopher menus and displays them in a new menu.

Veronica Very Easy Rodent Oriented Net-wide Index to Computerized Archives. An Internet service that searches for one or more keywords in Gopher menus.

Rather than running on your PC, you can connect to Veronica through a Gopher client program, such as WS Gopher. Many Gopher servers include one or more menu items with names like "Search Titles Using Veronica."

In this exercise, you will use Veronica to search for information about the composer Beethoven.

HANDS ON

1. Select the **New Gopher** command in the File Menu.

2. Move your cursor to the **Server Name** field and type **gopher.uiuc.edu**

   The main University of Illinois Gopher menu will appear.

3. Scroll down toward the bottom of the menu and double-click on **Other Gopher and Information Servers**.

   The menu in Figure 5-11 will appear.

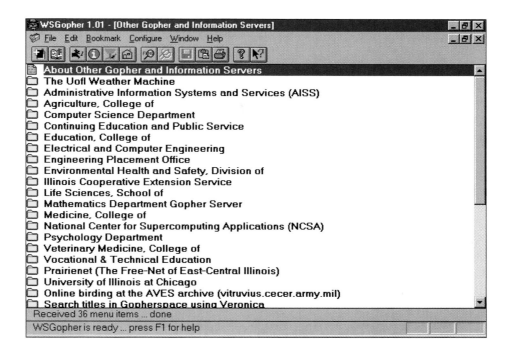

FIGURE 5-11

The Other Servers menu at
the University of Illinois

4. Scroll about halfway down the menu and double-click on the **Search titles in Gopherspace using Veronica** item.

The menu in Figure 5-12 will appear.

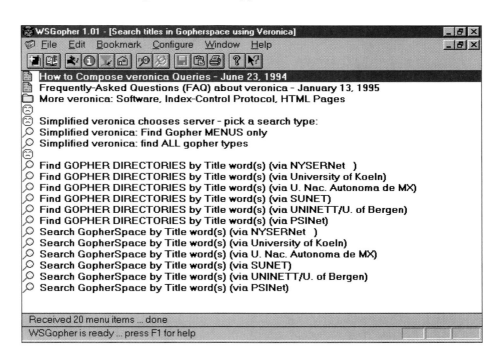

FIGURE 5-12

The list of Veronica servers
in the Illinois Other
Servers menu

5. Scroll down to the bottom of the menu and double-click on one of the **Search GopherSpace by Title word(s)** items.

The dialog box in Figure 5-13 will appear.

FIGURE 5-13

*The Search by Title
Words dialog box*

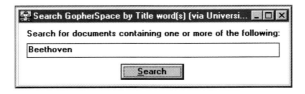

6. Type **Beethoven** in the **Search** field and click on the Search button.

WS Gopher will connect to the Gopher server you selected, and search for items with the word "Beethoven" in their titles. When the search is complete, a menu similar to the one in Figure 5-14 will appear, with a long list of files related to the famous composer.

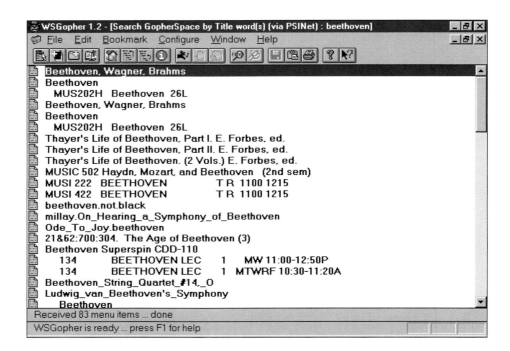

FIGURE 5-14

*The result of a Veronica
search for "Beethoven"*

In some cases, Veronica might find several hundred or more matches. You can treat an item from a search results menu in exactly the same way as an entry in any other Gopher menu: you can retrieve an item by double-clicking on it, or add it to your bookmark list.

LESSON SUMMARY AND EXERCISES

After completing this lesson, you should know how to do the following:

ABOUT GOPHER

- Gopher organizes Internet resources into menus and submenus.

NAVIGATING THROUGH GOPHERSPACE

- To navigate through Gopherspace, you must use a program called a Gopher client.

- To change fonts in WS Gopher, use the Fonts command in the Configure menu.

- Each item in a Gopher menu has an icon that identifies its type.

- To select an item from a Gopher menu, double-click on it.

JUMPING TO A SPECIFIC GOPHER

- To jump directly to a specific Gopher menu or item, use the New Gopher command in the File menu.

- To save the location of a Gopher menu or item, use the Add Bookmark command in the Bookmark menu.

- To change the Home Gopher menu that WS Gopher displays when you start the program, use the Home Gopher Server command in the Configure menu.

MORE AND BETTER INFORMATION WITH GOPHER+

- Gopher+ menus include additional information not included in Gopher plain menus.

- Extended Gopher+ information may include more detailed descriptions and alternate versions of a menu item.

- Ask Form opens a dialog box that requests information from the user before sending a file.

SEARCHING FOR GOPHER RESOURCES

- To use Veronica to search for an item in Gopherspace, find a Gopher menu that includes "Search Titles Using Veronica" as a menu item.

NEW TERMS TO REMEMBER

After completing this lesson, you should know the meaning of these terms:

Ask Form	Gopher+
extended information	Gopherspace
Gopher	Home Gopher
Gopher client	Veronica
Gopher server	

MATCHING EXERCISE

Match each of the terms with the definitions on the right:

TERMS	DEFINITIONS

1. Gopher

2. Gopherspace

3. Gopher client

4. Gopher server

5. Menu

6. Home Gopher

7. Gopher+

8. extended information

9. Ask Form

10. Veronica

a. The system of organizing Internet resources into menus and submenus

b. Additional details about an item in a Gopher+ menu

c. A program that permits a user to move among Gopher menus

d. A dialog box that requests information from a user before sending an item

e. A computer that contains one or more Gopher menus

f. That portion of the Internet that is organized into Gopher menus

g. A list of Internet resources

h. The Gopher menu that appears when you start your Gopher client program

i. The advanced version of Gopher that includes additional information about each item in its menus

j. A tool for searching through Gopherspace for specific items

COMPLETION EXERCISE

Fill in the missing word or phrase for each of the following statements:

1. Gopher organizes Internet resources into _____.

2. To jump to an item in a Gopher menu, _____ on it.

3. To save the location of a Gopher menu, create a _____ for that menu.

4. The Gopher menu that appears when you start a Gopher client is called the _____.

5. Items in Gopher+ menus have _____.

6. Look for a _____ item in a menu to search Gopherspace for specific resources.

7. WS Gopher is a _____ program.

8. The Gopher system originated at _____.

9. To jump directly to a specific Gopher menu in WS Gopher, use the _____ command.

SHORT-ANSWER QUESTIONS

Write a brief answer to each of the following questions:

1. How do you select an item from a Gopher menu?

2. Where would you start a Veronica search?

3. Explain how you would get to the Gopher menu at the University of Indiana.

4. How do you change the display fonts in WS Gopher?

5. Assume you found a Gopher menu that you want to return to in the future. How would you do it?

6. Where is the "Mother Gopher" that contains a registry of all other Gopher menus?

APPLICATION PROJECTS

Perform the following actions to complete these projects:

1. Starting at the University of Illinois' Gopher main menu, jump to *Other Gopher and Information Services*, and from there to the *Recommended Gopher Servers for Exploration* Gopher. Choose *United Nations* and then *The United Nations, what it is and what it does*. Finally, download a copy of the *Universal Declaration of Human Rights*.

2. Jump to the Virtual Reference Desk Gopher at *peg.cwis.uci.edu*. Select the *Foreign Currency Exchange Rates* menu item and find the current rates of exchange for the Canadian Dollar and the Italian Lira.

3. The University of Calgary in Alberta, Canada, is the home of the *Polar Information Sources* Gopher. Under *Other Polar Internet Sources*, there's a document called *Agreement on Conservation of Polar Bears*. Find it and print a copy of the agreement.

4. Use WS Gopher to obtain a satellite image of the United States.

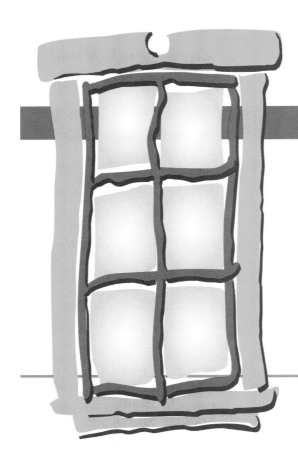

LESSON 6

BROWSING THE WORLD WIDE WEB

OBJECTIVES

After completing this lesson, you will be able to do the following:

- *Understand how the World Wide Web is organized.*
- *Move around Web pages and other hypertext documents.*
- *Use a World Wide Web browser.*
- *Use Universal Resource Locators.*

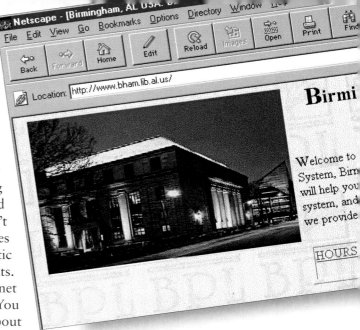

W hen you place a telephone call, you really don't care how the telephone company moves your voice to its destination—as long as the recipient can understand what you have to say, it doesn't matter whether the call goes through copper wires, fiber optic cable, or microwave radio circuits. In an ideal world, the Internet would work the same way. You wouldn't have to worry about choosing a telnet client for one function and Gopher for another.

A BOUT THE WORLD WIDE WEB

World Wide Web An Internet service that organizes information into hypertext documents.

In earlier chapters, you've learned about several quite different methods for moving information and other resources through the Internet to your PC. You're probably less interested in the data transfer method than the content of the data being transferred. The **World Wide Web** is a step in that direction.

The World Wide Web is a method for organizing all of the information on the Internet into a seamless system that uses links to move between individual documents or places within documents. You can use a World Wide Web browser program to transfer almost any kind of Internet resource back to your own computer. Therefore, you can concentrate on the content of the things you find online, rather than the programs needed to find them. Figure 6-1 shows a document in the Netscape Navigator browser.

The World Wide Web was created in 1989 at the European Particle Physics Laboratory in Geneva, Switzerland, as a scientific tool for distributing technical information. Until 1994, it was used almost exclusively by research centers and academic institutions.

Shortly after it was introduced in 1993, a program called Mosaic changed the way that many people use the Internet, and drastically increased the popularity of the entire system. Mosaic was created at the National Center for Supercomputing Applications (NCSA) at the University of Illinois, as the first Web browsing tool.

Web page A document that may be reached through the World Wide Web, and is formatted in Hypertext Markup Language (HTML).

Information on the World Wide Web is presented on **Web pages**, which may include both text and graphic images. Like a page in a book or a magazine, the layout of a Web page is limited only by the imagination of the designer.

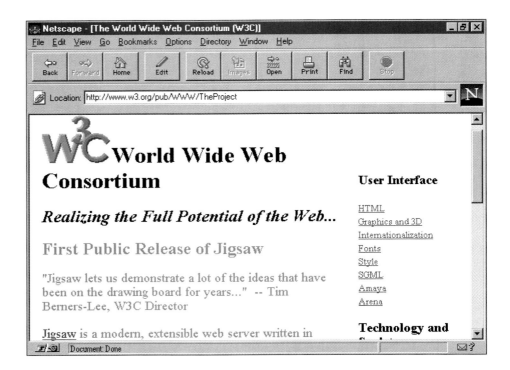

FIGURE 6-1

A World Wide Web document

hypertext A method of displaying information in which links to other documents and other Internet resources are embedded in the text of a document.

Hypertext Transfer Protocol (HTTP) The set of rules that defines the way hypertext links control the World Wide Web.

Hypertext Markup Language (HTML) The rules for creating World Wide Web documents with links to other resources.

Web browser An application program that downloads World Wide Web pages through the Internet and displays them on a computer.

The Web uses a format called **hypertext** to provide links between resources that may be located anywhere on the Internet. If you've spent any time using Windows Help, you're familiar with hypertext. Hypertext is an easy-to-use method for linking related information together. A hypertext jump may take you to another paragraph of the same document or a file halfway around the world.

Like the items in a Gopher menu, hypertext links may be pointers to any kind of Internet resources including other hypertext documents; text and data files; program files; and FTP, telnet, or Gopher servers. In other words, a hypertext jump can take you to just about anything on the Internet.

Unlike Gopher, where jumps are organized into formal menus, a hypertext link may be anywhere on your screen; it might be a word or a block of text, a picture, or a location on a map. Therefore, the appearance of a hypertext page can be whatever the creator wants it to look like.

The rules for hypertext pages are called **Hypertext Transfer Protocol (HTTP)**, using a page description format called **Hypertext Markup Language (HTML)**. Taken as a group, Internet resources that use hypertext are called the World Wide Web; the tools you use to read them are called **Web browsers**.

Netscape Navigator A Web browser program with a point-and-click graphical interface.

In this lesson, you will use a Web browser called **Netscape Navigator**. Netscape Navigator was created by Marc Andreessen, creator of the NCSA Mosaic browser software, and Dr. James H. Clark, founder of Silicon Graphics. In April 1994, they teamed up to form Mosaic Communications Corporation. By the beginning of 1995, their new and improved Web browser, Netscape Navigator, had been released, and the company changed its name to Netscape Communications Corporation. Today, Netscape is considered one of the greatest commercial successes in the Internet world.

INSTALLING NETSCAPE NAVIGATOR

If Netscape Navigator hasn't already been loaded on your computer, your instructor will give you a copy of the program.

WINDOWS 95 INSTALLATION

If your PC is using Windows 95, follow these steps to install Netscape Navigator:

HANDS ON

1. Create a new folder on your hard drive called **Netscape Install**.

   Your instructor will tell you the name of the file (usually N32E20.exe) that contains the Netscape software, which you will copy onto your hard drive.

2. Copy that file to the **Netscape Install** folder on your hard drive.

3. Use **Windows Explorer** to run the Netscape file in the **Netscape Install** folder.

   This is a self-extracting archive that contains several files.

4. When the extraction process is complete, run the **Setup** file now in the **Netscape Install** folder.

   Setup will install Netscape Navigator to a new folder on your hard drive (usually **Program Files/Netscape**).

STARTING THE PROGRAM

After installation is complete, Netscape Navigator should be ready to run.

HANDS ON

1. In Windows 95, use the Start Menu to choose the **Programs** command, then choose **Netscape**, then click on **Netscape Navigator**.

   Netscape Navigator will open and connect to the Netscape Home Page, shown in Figure 6-2.

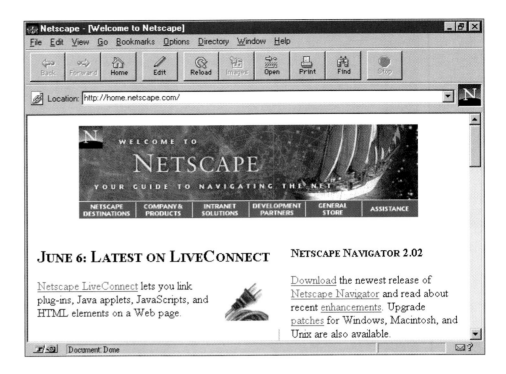

FIGURE 6-2

*The Netscape Navigator
Home Page*

2. Click on the **Maximize button.**

Now, you are ready to begin browsing the Web.

MOVING AROUND THE WEB

home page
1. A World Wide Web page used as a starting point for web browsing. 2. A World Wide Web page used by an information provider with pointers to related Internet resources.

HANDS ON

jump The process of using a hypertext link or Gopher menu item to connect to a new Internet resource.

link A dynamic pointer to an Internet resource. When you click on a link, your computer downloads the resource identified in the pointer.

A **home page** is a starting point for navigating through the World Wide Web. It generally has links to other resources that the creators of the home page think a reader might find useful or entertaining. In this exercise, you will start your Web explorations.

Notice that some of the text on your screen is in blue and underlined. These words or phrases are called **jumps** or **links**. A link may be a pointer to another section of the same web page, another file on the same host computer, or a file on some other computer half way around the world. Your cursor will change from an arrow to a pointing finger when you run your mouse over a link. Pictures can also represent links.

1. On the Netscape Home Page, click on the picture link to **Netscape Destinations.**

Netscape will download and display the **Destinations** Web page. While the file transfer is in progress, the animated Netscape logo at the upper-right corner of your screen is showered with meteors. When this animation stops, the file transfer is done or there has been an interruption in the connection. The message area in the bottom left of your screen will read **Document: Done** when the file has been successfully transferred.

2. Click on the **Travel** link. The Netscape Destinations Travel page is displayed, as shown in Figure 6-3.

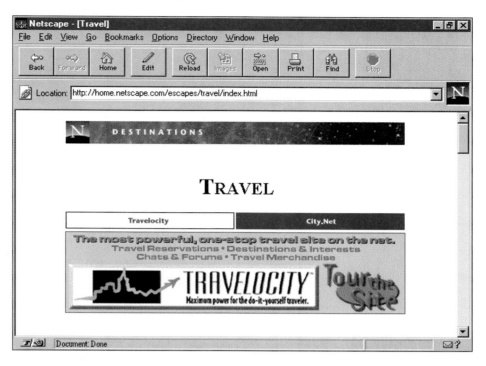

FIGURE 6-3
The Travel page

3. There are two travel services offered by Netscape. Click on **city.net** to activate its animation in the large frame.

4. In the large frame, click **city.net**. The city.net page is displayed (see Figure 6-4).

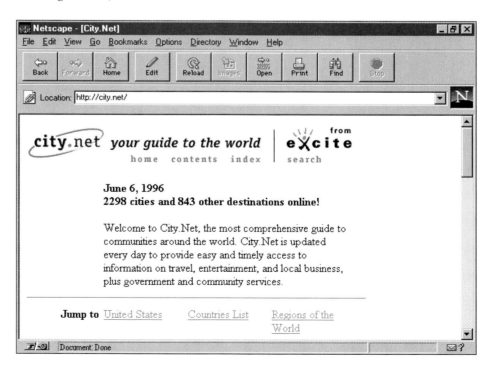

FIGURE 6-4
The city.net page

5. Next, scroll down to **Most Popular U.S. City Destinations,** click on **Atlanta** (see Figure 6-5).

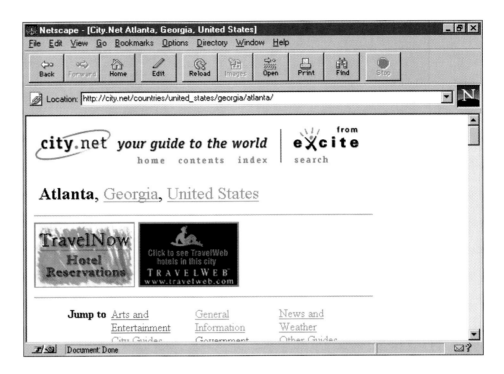

FIGURE 6-5

The city.net Atlanta page

6. Next to **Jump to,** click on the category **Government.** Then click on **City of Atlanta Home Page.** As in Figure 6-6, Netscape brings you to the City of Atlanta Home Page.

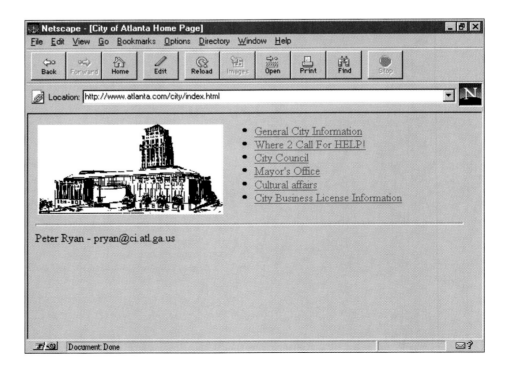

FIGURE 6-6

The City of Atlanta Home Page

USING URLS AND SEARCH ENGINES TO LINK TO WEB SITES

Tens of thousands of information providers have created Web pages, and new ones appear every week. Unlike Gopher, the Web doesn't have the kind of well-organized structure that allows you to move from any page to any other page in three or four steps. There are two ways to get around this problem: you can use one of the online directory services, or you can specify the exact address of a site you want to move to.

Uniform Resource Locators (URLs) are a special form of Internet addresses that are recognized by Web browsers. As the World Wide Web becomes more and more popular, you will see URLs in newspapers, magazines, and online discussions as pointers to resources on the Internet.

A URL has this format:

type://address/path

■ *Type* identifies the kind of Internet resource which might be HTTP (hypertext transfer protocol) for a Web page, FTP, telnet, Gopher, mail, or one of several other less common varieties.

■ Both the colon (:) and the two forward slashes (//) are essential parts of every URL. Your Web browser won't recognize a URL without them.

■ The *address* and *path* specify the exact location of a URL.

When you use a URL, you must make sure you copy it character for character. If even a single letter or punctuation mark is wrong, you won't be able to make the connection.

In this exercise, you will use the **Location** function in Netscape to jump to a very extensive Web search engine called **Yahoo. Yahoo** (Yet Another Hierarchical Organized Oracle) was created by two Stanford University students and has become one of the one of the most successful sites on the World Wide Web. Once in Yahoo, you will use the searching features to locate two museums, one in San Francisco and one in New York City.

Uniform Resource Locator (URL) A standard format for identifying the location and name of a file or other resource on the Internet. The World Wide Web uses URLs to identify links.

**HANDS
ON**

1. From the **City of Atlanta Home Page,** click on the Netscape menu item
File, then click **Open Location** (see Figure 6-7). The **Open Location** dialog appears, as shown in Figure 6-8.

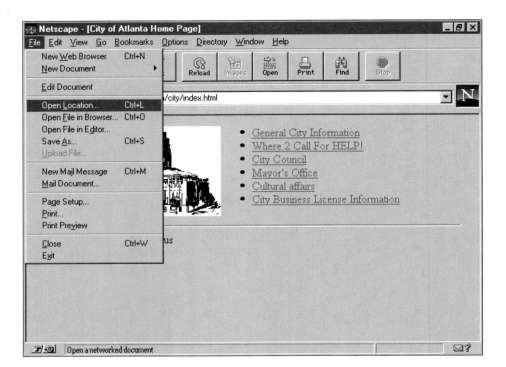

FIGURE 6-7
*Click **File**, then click*
Open Location

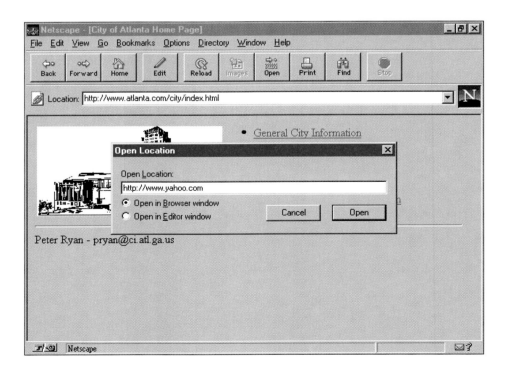

FIGURE 6-8
The Open Location
dialog box

2. In the text box, type in the Uniform Resource Locator for Yahoo **http://www.yahoo.com**. Then click **Open**. Netscape will load the Yahoo Home Page (see Figure 6-9).

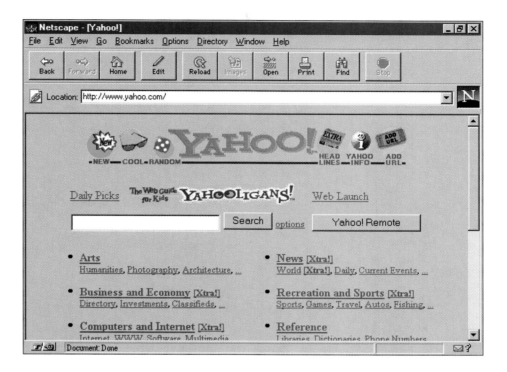

FIGURE 6-9

The Yahoo Home Page

Yahoo includes various search categories linked to thousands of Web pages.

3. Click on the **Arts** category link.

4. Scroll down to the **Museums and Galleries** link. Notice the number in parentheses after this link. It indicates the number of items in that sub-category. Click on **Museums and Galleries**.

The **Museums and Galleries** page appears (see Figure 6-10).

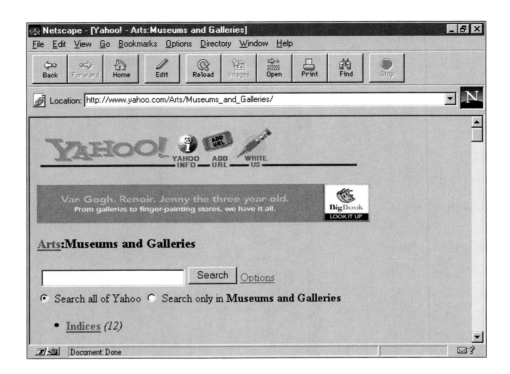

FIGURE 6-10
The Museums and
Galleries *page*

5. Scroll down to and click on the **California Palace of the Legion of Honor** link.

You are now linked to the California Palace of the Legion of Honor museum in San Francisco (see Figure 6-11). You can scroll down the page to view current exhibits and information about the museum.

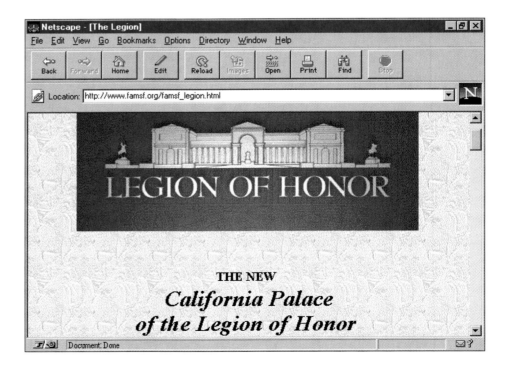

FIGURE 6-11
*The California Palace
of the Legion of Honor
Home Page*

Yahoo provides other ways to access Web sites. You can type in words and phrases, and Yahoo will search all its categories for matches.

HANDS ON

1. From the **California Palace of the Legion of Honor** page, click the Netscape **Back** button on the toolbar, or right click (in Windows 95) and select **Back**.

   This feature brings you to the previous page you viewed, in this case the Yahoo **Museums and Galleries** page.

2. Scroll up to the Search text box, and type in **Cooper Hewitt**. This is the name of the museum you will locate (see Figure 6-12). Notice that you can search all of Yahoo or just the Museums and Galleries category. Click **Search**.

   The Search Results page is displayed.

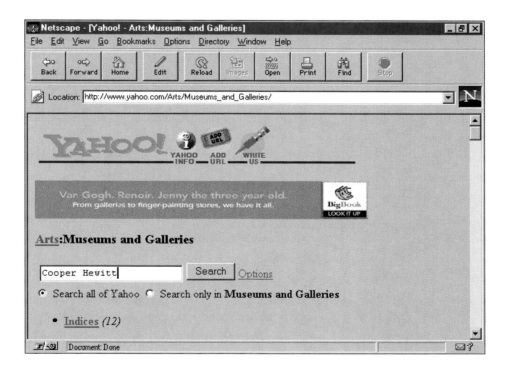

FIGURE 6-12

The Yahoo Search text box

3. Click on **Cooper-Hewitt**. The Cooper-Hewitt National Design Museum Home Page is displayed (see Figure 6-13).

FIGURE 6-13
The Cooper-Hewitt
National Design Museum
Home Page

SING BOOKMARKS

Bookmarks in Netscape Navigator are similar to the ones in WS Gopher. Bookmarks are Web site placeholders you can create based on your favorite sites. Bookmarks are stored as a list in a bookmark file on your hard drive. In this exercise, you will add a bookmark.

HANDS ON

1. From the **Cooper-Hewitt** Home Page, Click the menu item **Bookmarks**. Then click, **Add Bookmark**, as shown in Figure 6-14.

You have now added this location to your Bookmarks list. At any time, you can click **Bookmarks**, and then **Cooper-Hewitt**, and Netscape will take you directly to that page.

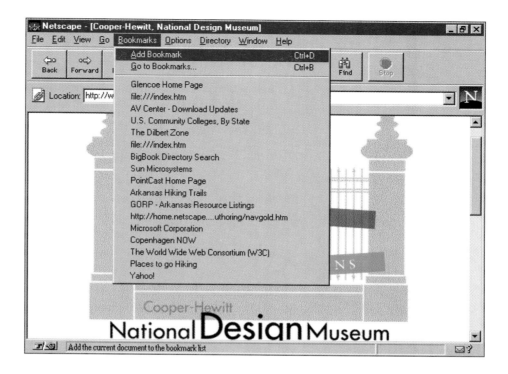

FIGURE 6-14
The **Bookmarks** *menu*

ETSCAPE NAVIGATOR COMMAND SUMMARY

The Netscape Navigator menu bar has nine menus. Here is a summary of the most commonly used menu bar commands. Many of these commands are duplicated in the toolbar.

FILE MENU

■ **Web Browser** This command creates a new Netscape window.

■ **New Mail Message** Use **New Mail Message** to create and send a new mail message over the Internet.

■ **Mail Document...** This command lets you create and send a mail message in the Message Composition window with the current page automatically attached. The content field contains the page's URL, and the subject field contains the page's title.

■ **Open Location...** Use this command to enter a URL.

■ **Open File...** Use the Open File command to display a file stored on your own computers' hard drive or diskette.

■ **Save As...** Use this command to save a copy of the current Web page in plain text format or in source (HTML format).

■ **Upload File...** This feature lets you select a file to upload to the FTP server specified by the current URL. This commands is only active when the current page accesses an FTP site. Permission is required.

■ **Page Setup...** This command lets you specify the printing characteristics of the current page.

■ **Print** Use this command to print the current Web page.

■ **Print Preview** Use the Print Preview command to see what a printed copy of the current page will look like.

■ **Close** This commands closes the current page.

■ **Exit** This command exits Netscape Navigator.

EDIT MENU

The commands in Netscape Navigator's Edit menu are similar to edit commands in many other Windows programs. You can use these commands to move text between Navigator and any other Windows application.

■ **Undo** This command reverses the last action you performed in Netscape Navigator.

■ **Cut...** Cut removes the current selection and places it on the Windows Clipboard.

■ **Copy** This command places a copy of the current selection on the Windows Clipboard.

■ **Paste** Use **Paste** to place the contents of the Clipboard into the current Netscape Navigator page at the position of the cursor.

■ **Select All** This commands highlights all of the text in the current Web page. Combined with the **Copy** command, you can use **Select All** to copy the text of a Web page to your word processing program or some other Windows application.

■ **Find...** Use the **Find** command to search for a word or character string in the current Web page.

■ **Find Again** This command searches for another occurrence of the text specified in **Find**.

VIEW MENU

■ **Reload** This command brings a fresh copy of the current Netscape page to replace the one originally loaded.

■ **Reload Frame** This command brings a fresh copy of the currently selected page within a single frame on a Netscape page containing frames.

- **Load Images** Use **Load Images** to display the images of the current Web page. Typically, images automatically load into pages. If they don't, use this command.

- **Refresh** This command brings a fresh copy of the current Web page from local memory to replace the one originally loaded.

- **Document Source** This command produces a View Source window showing the current page in HTML code.

- **Document Info** Use this command to view the current page's structure and composition including title, location (URL), date of last modification, character set encoding, and security status.

GO MENU

The Go menu contains commands that tell Netscape Navigator to load different Web pages.

- **Back** This command displays the previous page.

- **Forward** Use **Forward** to display the next page in memory.

- **Home** This command displays the default home page, usually Netscape's.

- **Stop Loading** Use this command to halt the process of loading a Web page.

- *History Items* The Go menu appends the title of each Web page you access to the history list at the bottom of the menu. At any time, you can choose a Web page title from this list to display it.

HELP MENU

Most of the commands in the **Help** menu are links to the Netscape Navigator's online Handbook.

TOOLBAR BUTTONS

Netscape Navigator's toolbar contains ten icon buttons shown in Figure 6-15. All of the toolbar commands duplicate commands in the menus. When you move the cursor over an icon button, a "Tool Tip" appears that explains that button.

Toolbar ——

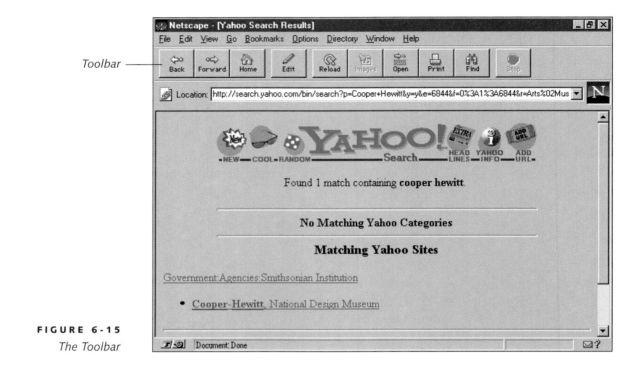

FIGURE 6-15
The Toolbar

EXPLORING THE WEB

Now that you have learned the basic methods needed to move around the World Wide Web, the best way to learn what the Web has to offer is to spend some time exploring the Web on your own. Click on a topic in the Yahoo menu that sounds interesting, and follow the links to see where they take you.

LESSON SUMMARY AND EXERCISES

After completing this lesson, you should know how to do the following:

ABOUT THE WORLD WIDE WEB

- The World Wide Web organizes Internet resources that use different protocols under a common interface.
- The Web's native format uses hypertext jumps to other resources.
- Hypertext links may be anywhere on a page.

INSTALLING NETSCAPE NAVIGATOR

- To install Netscape Navigator, copy the Netscape file to your hard drive, run the self-extracting file, and then run the Setup program.

MOVING AROUND THE WEB

- To use a link on a Web page, click on the word or image that describes the link.

USING URLS AND SEARCH ENGINES TO LINK TO WEB SITES

- To jump to a new location, type the URL in the white field directly under the toolbar and click on the green check mark.

USING BOOKMARKS

- To add a site to your list, use the Add Bookmark command in the Bookmarks menu.

NETSCAPE NAVIGATOR COMMAND SUMMARY

- The commands in the menu bar manage files, open URLs, and control the appearance of the screen.
- The toolbar buttons provide fast and easy access to many commands.

EXPLORING THE WEB

- The best way to learn about the World Wide Web is to spend some time exploring it.

NEW TERMS TO REMEMBER

After completing this lesson, you should know the meaning of these terms:

home page	link
hypertext	Netscape Navigator
Hypertext Markup Language (HTML)	Uniform Resource Locator (URL)
Hypertext Transfer Protocol (HTTP)	Web browser
jump	Web page
	World Wide Web

MATCHING EXERCISE

Match each of the terms with the definitions on the right:

TERMS	DEFINITIONS
1. World Wide Web	**a.** Move to a new file or Internet host, or to a different part of the same document by clicking on a word, phrase or graphic image
2. hypertext	
3. Hypertext Transfer Protocol (HTTP)	**b.** The rules that apply to World Wide Web documents
4. Hypertext Markup Language (HTML)	**c.** A tool for displaying HTML documents and navigating the World Wide Web
5. Web browser	**d.** A Web browser program
6. Netscape Navigator	**e.** The system that organizes the Internet into hypertext links
7. home page	
8. jump	**f.** A word, phrase or graphic element of a Web page that moves the user to another Internet resource
9. link	
10. URL	**g.** The text format that embeds links to other Internet resources or other parts of the same document into an online test file
	h. The identity of a file, host computer, or other Internet resource
	i. A Web page with links to other Internet resources, used as a starting point for Web browsing
	j. Text that contains words or phrases that are links to other documents or files, or to other parts of the same document

COMPLETION EXERCISE

Fill in the missing word or phrase for each of the following statements:

1. A program that displays HTML pages and supports links to other Internet resources is called a _____.

2. To move to a new Web page or other Internet resource, type the _____ that identifies the resource in the field under the toolbar.

3. The page description format used for Web pages is _____.

4. To save the URL of a Web page or other Internet resource in Netscape, add the URL to your _____.

5. The _____ command returns you to the Web page you displayed just before the current screen.

6. To return to your home page, click on the toolbar button with _____ on it.

7. When the Netscape logo in the upper-right corner of the Netscape screen is animated, it indicates _____.

8. To use a link in an HTML document _____ on it.

APPLICATION PROJECTS

Perform the following actions to complete these projects:

1. The home page for United States government's FedWorld Information Network is at *http://www.fedworld.gov*. You can jump from FedWorld to many other online information sources offered by various government agencies.

   Open the FedWorld home page. In the list of subject categories, select *Agriculture and Food*. From the Agriculture page, choose the link to the page with information about the Gypsy Moth in North America. Print a copy of the Gypsy Moth page.

2. Use the Lycos Web search tool at *http://www.lycos.com* to look for *Blacksburg Electronic Village*. The Blacksburg Electronic Village (BEV) from Blacksburg, Virginia, will be the first or second item in the list of Web pages that match the search terms. Click on the link to BEV, and jump from there to the Welcome Page. Print a copy of the Blacksburg Welcome page.

3. Quantum Corporation is a manufacturer of disk drives for personal computers. They maintain a Web page at *http://www.quantum.com* which displays news and sales information about their products. Use Netscape's Open URL command to display the Quantum home page. Choose the link to *Corporate and Financial Information* from the list under *Welcome to Quantum Corporation*, and then jump to the corporate fact sheet. Print a copy of the fact sheet.

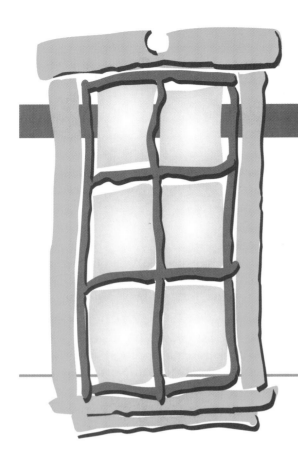

INTERNET UTILITIES

OBJECTIVES

After completing this lesson, you will be able to do the following:

- *Use Ping to check the status of an Internet host.*
- *Use Finger to obtain information about other Internet users.*
- *Obtain information from a Finger server.*
- *Use Archie to locate files in FTP archives.*

CONTENTS

Login name: magliaco
Directory: /njin/u4/magliaco
Last login Wed Aug 16 22:02 on ttyrd from quinc
No unread mail
Project: Feel free to visit my home page at: h
Plan:

****
* SpaceNews is available via the Amateur Pac
* via the AMSAT-OSCAR-16 and LUSAT-OSCAR-19
* also posted to Usenet under the newsgroups
* rec.radio.info, and sci.space.news. Arch
* anonymous FTP at pilot.njin.net in the pu
****

And now for the news...

SB NEWS @ AMSAT $SPC0814
* SpaceNews 14-Aug-95 *

BID: $SPC0814

T he Internet can fall victim to the same kind of problems that all other computers have: it doesn't always work the way you want it to work. Sometimes you may try to connect to a distant host, and get an error message instead of a login. In other cases, you may want to find more information about an Internet user or a host computer before you try to set up a connection or send a message.

This chapter includes information about a tool that you can use to confirm that you can actually reach another host, a tool for obtaining information about other Internet users, and a search tool for locating files in FTP archives.

USING PING TO TEST INTERNET CONNECTIONS

Ping An Internet service for testing connections between computers. It sends an echo request to a distant computer and measures the amount of time needed to receive a reply.

Ping is a utility that measures the amount of time it takes to send a round-trip message between two computers on the Internet. The word "Ping" is an abbreviation of Packet InterNet Groper, but it's also a good description of the way Ping works. Ping is the name of the program, but it's also used as a verb, so a network system administrator might ask you to "try Pinging a host."

Remember all those movies about submarines where they send high-pitched "pinging" sounds to find the battleship on the surface? The sonar operator measures the amount of time it takes for the sound to return and uses that information to figure out how far away the target is located. On the Internet, Ping works the same way. You send a request for acknowledgment to another computer and measure the time it takes to receive a reply. The Ping utility tells you that it has received an acknowledgment and how long it took.

This is useful information. It tells you that you are able to successfully connect your own computer to the Internet, that the distant host is active and connected to the Internet, and something about the quality of the connection.

WS Ping is a free program that sends Ping requests through Winsock connections.

Here's how to start WS Ping in Windows 95:

HANDS ON

1. Click on the Start button to open the Windows 95 Start menu.

2. Open the Programs, **Internet Tools** menu.

3. Select the **WS Ping** command to open the window in Figure 7-1.

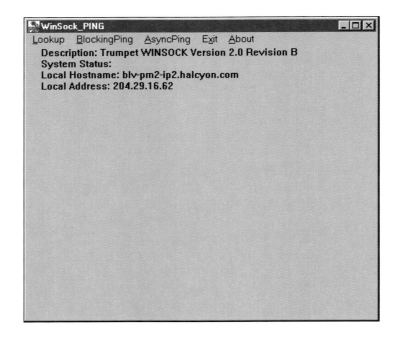

FIGURE 7-1

The Winsock Ping window

If you're using Windows 3.X, follow these steps to start WS Ping:

HANDS ON

1. If it's not already visible, open the **Internet Tools** program group.

2. Double-click on the WS Ping icon.

When the WS Ping window in Figure 7-1 appears, follow these steps to send a Ping request to a computer at the University of Washington in Seattle:

HANDS ON

1. Click on **AsyncPing** in the menu bar to open the Host dialog box shown in Figure 7-2.

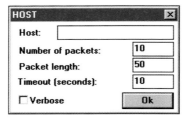

FIGURE 7-2

*The Winsock Ping
Host dialog box*

2. Type **u.washington.edu** in the **Host** field and click the OK button.

This command sends ten Ping requests to a computer at the University of Washington in Seattle. When the test is complete, WS Ping will display statistics about the number of successful tests, and the shortest, average, and longest amount of time needed to receive an answer from the computer in Seattle. Figure 7-3 shows a Ping Statistics report.

3. Click on the Close button in the menu bar to close WS Ping.

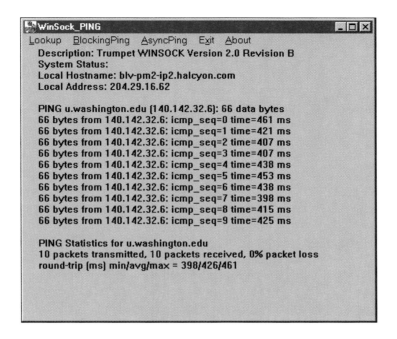

WinSock_PING
Lookup BlockingPing AsyncPing Exit About
Description: Trumpet WINSOCK Version 2.0 Revision B
System Status:
Local Hostname: blv-pm2-ip2.halcyon.com
Local Address: 204.29.16.62

PING u.washington.edu (140.142.32.6): 66 data bytes
66 bytes from 140.142.32.6: icmp_seq=0 time=461 ms
66 bytes from 140.142.32.6: icmp_seq=1 time=421 ms
66 bytes from 140.142.32.6: icmp_seq=2 time=407 ms
66 bytes from 140.142.32.6: icmp_seq=3 time=407 ms
66 bytes from 140.142.32.6: icmp_seq=4 time=438 ms
66 bytes from 140.142.32.6: icmp_seq=5 time=453 ms
66 bytes from 140.142.32.6: icmp_seq=6 time=438 ms
66 bytes from 140.142.32.6: icmp_seq=7 time=398 ms
66 bytes from 140.142.32.6: icmp_seq=8 time=415 ms
66 bytes from 140.142.32.6: icmp_seq=9 time=425 ms

PING Statistics for u.washington.edu
10 packets transmitted, 10 packets received, 0% packet loss
round-trip (ms) min/avg/max = 398/426/461

FIGURE 7-3

A Ping report from u.washington.edu

You can use WS Ping to run three different tests: Blocking Ping, Non-Blocking (Asynchronous) Ping, and Lookup. The Blocking and Asynchronous tests usually produce similar results. The Lookup test obtains an IP address from your local name server, but it does not actually connect to the host.

If a Ping request fails, it could mean that you are not properly connected to the Internet. Therefore, it's a good way to make sure you have set up and configured your connection correctly. When your first Ping test fails, try Pinging another host. If that one works, you can be reasonably confident that the problem is not in your own set-up. If all of your Ping tests fail, it's time to check your network connection or call your system administrator or help desk.

When you run a Ping test, you usually send several Ping requests to the same destination, and calculate the average amount of time (in milliseconds) needed to receive a reply. However, you might not receive replies to every request. This is not a serious problem because the Internet uses a data transmission method that breaks the data stream into **packets**, which are relatively small bundles of data. If you lose an occasional packet when you're sending or receiving real data (rather than test packets), the originating system will automatically re-send lost packets.

If the average reply time is greater than about one second (1000 ms), there might be a problem somewhere between your computer and the distant host. There could be a lot of other users exchanging data with the same host, or the host might be using a low-speed connection to the Internet.

packet A bundle of data arranged in a carefully defined way for transmission across a communication circuit. A packet usually includes control information, the data itself, and error detection and correction information.

Finger An Internet service that returns a block of text from a server on request.

plan The block of text that a computer sends when it receives a Finger request.

The only thing you get back when you send a Ping request is a reply packet that is the digital equivalent to "Hello, I'm alive." If you want more specific information about a particular host, or about a specific user, you should use **Finger**.

A Finger request is an instruction to a host computer to send you a list of people who are currently using that computer. If you include the name of a user in your Finger request, the host will return some information about that user, including a block of text called a **plan**. A plan could be anything from information about the user's vacation schedule to a long and detailed news bulletin.

Since you don't have to formally log in to a system to Finger one of its users, some people use Finger as a way to post public information to anybody who might care to read it.

In this section, you will use a Finger program to see a list of currently active users on a distant system, details about an individual user, and a Finger server that reports on recent earthquake activity.

FINGERING A DISTANT HOST

Finger was originally used on mainframe computers where many people could be using the system at the same time. The Finger command would let you know who else was currently online. When people began connecting computers to networks, Finger extended across the network lines to let a user on one machine know who is using some other machine.

HANDS ON

1. Click on the Start button to open the Start menu.

2. Open the Programs, **Internet Tools** menu.

3. Select the **Finger** command to open the Finger window in Figure 7-4.

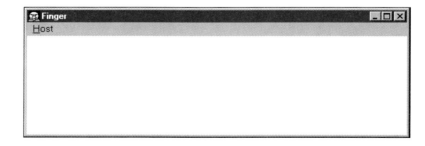

FIGURE 7-4
The Finger window as it first appears

4. Open the Host menu and select the **Host** command to open the dialog box in Figure 7-5.

5. Type **pilot.njin.net** in the **Enter A Host Name Or Internet Address** field and click the OK button.

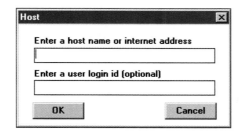

FIGURE 7-5

The Finger Host dialog box

Finger will obtain list of active users on *pilot.njin.net* at Rutgers University in New Jersey. Figure 7-6 shows a current user list display.

```
Finger - pilot.njin.net                                              _ 8 X
Host
Login        Name                TTY Idle      When     Where
latzko       Alex                ta     3 Thu 16:34  marsenius.rutger
shays        Sharon Hays         p1  8:25 Thu 08:12  shiloh.rutgers.e
ivyyew       Ivy Yew             p4       Thu 16:26  liza.st-elizabet
chrlee       Christopher Lee     pa       Thu 16:33  engelhard.rutger
daley        Michael Daley       pc    15: Thu 00:55  antietam:0.0
ehou         Edwin Hou           pd    31 Thu 15:55  basie.rutgers.ed
rharnaga     ???                 pe  3:12 Thu 11:31  clavius.rutgers.
phj          Patricia H. Ju      pf    10 Wed 14:51  reliant:S.0
phj          Patricia H. Ju      q0     4 Wed 14:52  reliant:S.1
idrogo       Curt Idrogo         q2    14 Thu 14:00  engelhard.rutger
llawton      Leora Lawton        *q3   8d Wed 12:10  parker.rutgers.e
latzko       Alex                qa  2:38 Thu 15:29  marsenius.rutger
rapatel      Rocky - Rakesh Patel qe   9d Tue 14:16  ptolemaeus.rutge
donur        Damoder Donur       r1       Thu 14:14  swiss.ans.net
thayes       Tim Hayes           r2  1:26 Wed 16:44  copernicus.rutge
giaimis      jeanne giaimis      r5     1 Thu 13:30  engelhard.rutger
phj          Patricia H. Ju      r7    11 Wed 15:06  reliant:S.2
selaya       Jose A. Selaya      ra     8 Thu 16:25  engelhard.rutger
nayang       ???                 rc  1:44 Thu 14:46  ua1vm.ua.edu
lostar       Lewis Ostar         rd    38 Thu 15:38  rvcc.raritanval.
gchamra      Gregg Chamra        re       Thu 16:17  basie.rutgers.ed
drummond     Walt Drummond       rf    6d Fri 13:09  aristarchus.rutg
spall        Aileen Spall        s4    5d Fri 16:16  149.152.45.243
wilinski     Grant Wilinski      s5  1:08 Thu 15:27  192.133.105.60
caddison     Cynthia Addison     s6       Thu 09:26  hoboken.dl.steve
dblack       David Alan Black    s8  1:31 Thu 14:10  candle.superlink
rharnaga     ???                 sa  1:13 Thu 10:50  clavius rutgers
```

FIGURE 7-6

*A Finger report for a host
at Rutgers University*

The top line of the Finger list contains a heading for each of the columns:

Login   The Login column lists the account name for each active user.

Name   The Name column shows each user's full name.

TTY   The TTY column shows the terminal or modem port that each person is using to connect to this host.

Idle   The Idle column lists the number of days, hours and minutes since the last time this user entered a command. If a user has been idle for a long time, that user may have gone home without breaking the connection to the host.

When   The When column shows the day and time that the current session started.

FINGERING AN INDIVIDUAL USER

When you Finger a single user, you get quite a different kind of report. Instead of a list of names, you see a lot of details about one person.

HANDS ON

1. Open the Host menu and select the **Host** command.

2. Type **pilot.njin.net** in the **Enter A Host Name Or Internet Address** field.

3. Type **magliaco** in the **Enter A User Login ID** field.

4. Click on the OK button.

The Finger program window will display the information in Figure 7-7.

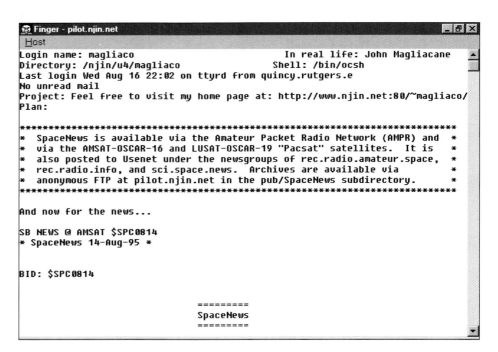

FIGURE 7-7
A Finger report for a user at Rutgers University

Finger reports on individual users generally include this information:

Login Name	A user's Login Name is the name that person uses to identify himself to the computer.
In Real Life	The Real Life name is the user's full name.
Phone	The Phone field contains the user's voice telephone number.
Directory and Shell	The Directory and Shell listings are not particularly interesting unless you're on the same system.
Last Login	The Last Login entry shows the time and date of this user's most recent connection to this system. This information can be confusing, because Finger sometimes reaches a user's mail server, rather than the computer they actually use every day.

Plan   The Plan field contains a block of text created by
                              the user. A Plan might be "Return from lunch at
                              1:15," or "Attend Susan's birthday party next Sat-
                              urday." Later in this section, you will see a Plan
                              that contains several paragraphs of useful infor-
                              mation.

SEARCHING FOR A USER

You can also use Finger when you know the name of the host somebody uses, but you're not sure about their login name.

HANDS ON

1. Open the Host menu and select the **Host** command.

2. Type **halcyon.com** in the **Enter A Host Name Or Internet Address** field.

3. Type **John** in the **Enter A User Login ID** field.

4. Click the OK button.

Finger will collect information about all of the people named John who
have accounts on holcyon.com. Figure 7-8 shows a collection set of Finger
data.

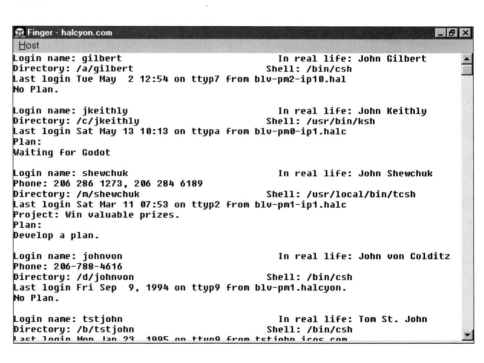

FIGURE 7-8

*The result of a
Finger search for
people named John*

OBTAINING INFORMATION FROM AN INFORMATION SERVER

There are many Finger servers on the Internet that have special accounts with blocks of information in their plans. For example, you might
find a football team's schedule, or the mailing address of a business.

One of the most unusual Finger servers is operated by the U. S. Geo-
logical Survey's National Earthquake Information Service.

HANDS ON

1. Open the Host menu and select the **Host** command.

2. Type **gldfs.cr.usgs.gov** in the **Enter A Host Name Or Internet Address** field.

3. Type **quake** in the **Enter A User Login ID** field.

4. Click the OK button.

A list of recent earthquakes around the world, similar to the one in Figure 7-9, will appear.

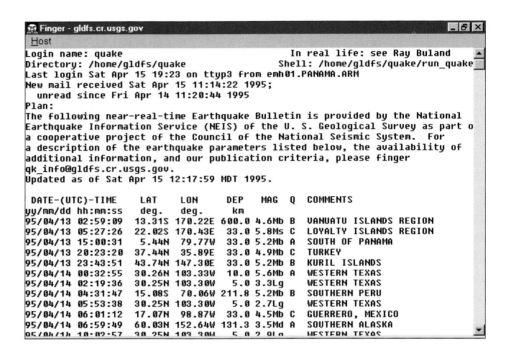

FIGURE 7-9

The USGS earthquake server

USING ARCHIE TO SEARCH FTP ARCHIVES

Archie An Internet service that searches through many FTP directories and returns a list of files (with their locations) that match a specified string of characters.

As you learned in Lesson 4, there are thousands of files stored in FTP archives all over the world that you can download to your own PC. **Archie** is a convenient way to search through all those separate archives.

Archie was created at McGill University in Montreal, Canada. It's called "Archie" because it's a super-archive of FTP servers. Once a month, the master Archie server in Montreal copies the directories from hundreds of other FTP archives. It stores a copy of the list, and sends copies to about two dozen other Archie servers around the world. To run an Archie search, send a request to one of the servers, with the full or partial name of the file you're looking for. The server compares the request to the latest directory of files, and returns a complete list of all the files that match the name in the original request. Since the list includes the address of each archive that contains matching files, you can use anonymous FTP to download a copy of the file you want.

Archie client A computer program that performs an Archie search.

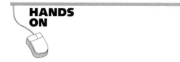

HANDS ON

To perform an Archie search, you need an **Archie client** program. In this lesson, you will use the Archie client program that's included in Netscape Navigator.

1. Click on the Start button and open **Netscape Navigator** from the Internet Tools submenu under the Programs menu.

2. Access the **Open Location** dialog box from the **File** menu.

3. Type in the URL **http://hoohoo.ncsa.uiuc.edu/archie.html**.

Netscape will download the Archie Request Form shown in Figure 7-10.

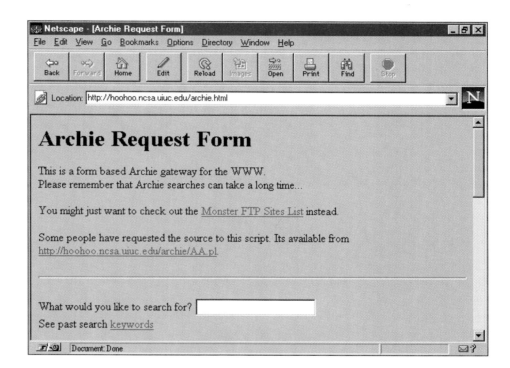

FIGURE 7-10

A World Wide Web Archie Request Form

4. Type **rabbit** in the **What Would You Like To Search For** field.

5. Move down to the **There Are Several Types Of Search** field and drop down the menu.

A list of Archie servers appears. All the servers contain identical lists of files, so you can choose any server from the list.

6. Click on the name of the server you want to use.

Don't change any of the other fields in the Archie form.

7. Click the Submit button.

Netscape will send your request to the Archie server you specified. It may take several minutes to get an answer. If you get no response after three or four minutes, try a different server. Eventually, Netscape will load a list of files which include the word "rabbit" in their names, including guitar music for the old Jefferson Airplane song called *White Rabbit*, a type font called "rabbit ears," pictures of assorted rabbits, a review of the movie *Who Framed Roger Rabbit?,* and several recipes, including one called "terrine lapin mon oncle rabbit," which roughly translates as "my Uncle Rabbit's cold rabbit meat loaf."

As you can see, you're likely to find many files you don't want along with the one you're really searching for. If you know the exact name of the file you want, you can usually home in on it more quickly than you could with a broad general term. For instance, if you had specified "white rabbit" instead of just "rabbit," you would only see a small fraction of the "rabbit" list.

Each item in the list is a link to the file it names. To download a copy of the file, click on the item. If you prefer, you can click on the address or the name of the host to see a directory of other files in the same FTP archive.

Many files exist in more than one FTP archive. Since there are only a limited number of Internet circuits across the Atlantic and Pacific oceans, you should try to download the file from an archive as close to home as possible. In North America, that generally means that if you have a choice, you should select an FTP archive with an address that ends in .edu, .com, .org, .net, or .ca (for Canada).

LESSON SUMMARY AND EXERCISES

After completing this lesson, you should know how to do the following:

USING PING TO TEST INTERNET CONNECTIONS

■ Ping sends a request for an echo across the Internet to a distant host.

■ The result of a Ping test tells you that your own computer is connected to the Internet, and that the distant host is on line.

USING FINGER TO GET INFORMATION FROM A HOST

■ A Finger request to a host produces a list of people who are currently using that host.

■ Fingering an individual user instructs that user's home computer to return information about that user.

■ Some information servers use Finger to distribute a block of information, such as a schedule or a report of recent activity.

USING ARCHIE TO SEARCH FTP ARCHIVES

■ Archie is a combined list of files located in many FTP archives around the world.

■ To use Archie to search for a file, send a request with a partial or complete file name to an Archie server.

NEW TERMS TO REMEMBER

After completing this lesson, you should know the meaning of these terms:

Archie	packet
Archie client	Ping
Finger	plan

MATCHING EXERCISE

Match each of the terms with the definitions on the right:

TERMS	DEFINITIONS
1. Ping	**a.** An Internet utility that retrieves information about users on a distant computer
2. Ping request	**b.** An Internet service for searching for a file in many FTP archives
3. Finger	
4. Finger server	**c.** A command to a distant computer to return an echo to the host
5. plan	
6. Archie	**d.** An Internet utility that sends echo requests to a distant host
7. Archie server	**e.** A block of information about a user that a host will forward in response to a Finger command
8. FTP Archive	
	f. A computer that returns information in response to a Finger request
	g. A collection of files that are available for free downloading across the Internet
	h. A computer that contains directories for hundreds of FTP archives

COMPLETION EXERCISE

Fill in the missing word or phrase for each of the following statements:

1. A Ping request measures the amount of _____ it takes to receive a reply.

2. To send a Ping request, you must specify the _____ of a host.

3. If a Ping request fails, it means _____.

4. Finger is a request for information about _____ at a distant host.

5. When you Finger an individual user, it returns a block of information called a _____.

6. A computer that returns information in response to a Finger request is a _____.

7. The utility that searches for files in FTP archives is _____.

8. To search for a file, send _____ to an Archie server.

9. When an Archie server returns a list of files, _____ on the name of a file to download it.

SHORT-ANSWER QUESTIONS

Write a brief answer to each of the following questions:

1. What does it mean if you receive no response to a Ping request?

2. How would you obtain a list of users currently logged on at a distant host?

3. What happens when you Finger an individual name?

4. How would you obtain somebody's e-mail address if you know their real name?

5. What kind of Internet resource does Archie search for?

6. How do you use Netscape Navigator to run an Archie search?

APPLICATION PROJECTS

Perform the following actions to complete these projects:

1. The University of Washington operates an earthquake activity reporting service on a Finger server whose address is *quake@geophys.washington .edu*. Use Finger to obtain a copy of the current report.

2. Send a Ping request to *well.com*. Copy the host's numeric IP address and the average time needed to receive echo packets.

3. There are several FTP archives of recipes. Perform an Archie search for "salmon" and download and print a recipe for salmon chowder.

3270 The model number of a widely-used IBM terminal. Many IBM mainframes require 3270 terminal emulation.

address The identity of a location on the Internet.

alias An easy-to-remember substitute you create for a complex or long name and address that an e-mail program then translates to an e-mail address or list of addresses. In Eudora, aliases are called "nicknames."

anonymous FTP The process of logging in to an FTP server where you don't have an account with the account name "anonymous" and your e-mail address as password.

Archie An Internet service that searches through many FTP directories and returns a list of files (with their locations) that match a specified string of characters.

Archie client A computer program that performs an Archie search.

Archie server A computer that contains copies of FTP directories from thousands of FTP sites.

article A message posted to a news group.

article window In Trumpet News, the window where the text of an article appears.

Ask Form A dialog box that requests information from the user.

client A computer that requests information or services from another computer through a network.

domain Part of an address that identifies the type of organization, such as .edu for education; or the part that identifies the geographical location of the addressee, such as .fr for France.

Domain Name Server A database that converts names to numbers, specifically Domain Name System addresses to numeric IP addresses.

Domain Name System The Internet address format identifies locations on the Internet by domains such as .edu, .org, and .fr.

driver A set of instructions in software which convert commands from an application program to the format required by a specific communications device.

dumb terminal A computer terminal with no built-in processing power.

e-mail The exchange of messages and computer files through the Internet and other electronic data networks. Short for "electronic mail."

e-mail address The name and location of an Internet (or other electronic communication service) user, such as *fredu@qcc.edu*.

extended information The information supplied by Gopher+.

FAQ Frequently Asked Questions. A set of questions and answers that contain introductory information about a specific subject.

Finger An Internet service that returns a block of text from a server on request.

FTP File Transfer Protocol. The Internet service that moves files between computers.

Gopher A system of linked menus with pointers to Internet resources and other menus. When a user selects an item from a menu, the Gopher client downloads a copy of the file or menu identified by that menu item.

Gopher+ An extended Gopher service that includes additional information about items in Gopher menus.

Gopher client A computer program that connects to Gopher servers, displays Gopher menus, and downloads resources listed in those menus.

Gopher server A computer that contains one or more Gopher menus.

Gopherspace That portion of the Internet that is accessible through Gopher menus.

header A block of information about an e-mail message that appears at the top of the message.

Home Gopher The Gopher menu that a Gopher client program uses as a starting point.

home page **1.** A World Wide Web page used as a starting point for web browsing. **2.** A World Wide Web page used by an information provider with pointers to related Internet resources.

hypertext A method of displaying information in which links to other documents and other Internet resources are embedded in the text of a document.

Hypertext Markup Language (HTML) The rules for creating World Wide Web documents with links to other resources.

Hypertext Transfer Protocol (HTTP) The set of rules that defines the way hypertext links control the World Wide Web.

Inbox A Eudora file that contains inbound e-mail messages.

Internet The Internet is the world-wide interconnected network of computers that can exchange messages, commands, and data.

IP Address Internet Protocol Address. An Internet address in numeric format.

jump The process of using a hypertext link or Gopher menu item to connect to a new Internet resource.

link A dynamic pointer to an Internet resource. When you click on a link, your computer downloads the resource identified in the pointer.

log in The process of entering a user's name and password into a computer, in order to start using the computer.

mail server A computer that processes electronic mail for client computers.

mailbox A storage area on a mail server where the server holds mail for an individual address until that subscriber's mail program downloads it.

mailing list An online discussion group that distributes articles by e-mail. When you send a message to the list server, it automatically distributes the message to all of the participants in the mailing list.

message queue A "holding area" for messages that Eudora or another mail manager program will upload to a mail server when a connection is established.

moderated news group A news group whose messages are reviewed by a "host" or "moderator" to assure that all messages are related to the news group's topic.

netiquette The body of commonly accepted rules for exchange of e-mail and news through the Internet and other electronic networks.

Netscape Navigator A Web browser program with a point-and-click graphical interface.

news The electronic exchange of public messages organized by subject.

news group A set of news articles about a single topic.

news reader An application program for sending and receiving online news articles.

news server A computer that supplies news articles to a news reader program.

nickname An alias in Eudora.

packet A bundle of data arranged in a carefully defined way for transmission across a communication circuit. A packet usually includes control information, the data itself, and error detection and correction information.

Ping An Internet service for testing connections between computers. It sends an echo request to a distant computer and measures the amount of time needed to receive a reply.

plan The block of text that a computer sends when it receives a Finger request.

PPP Point-to-Point Protocol. A data format used to connect a PC to the Internet.

protocol A set of signals and commands that computers use to communicate with one another.

remote terminal A terminal or other input and output device connected to a computer through the Internet or some other network.

server A computer that supplies data or services to a client.

shell account An account on a host computer that uses the host's command line interface to connect a PC as a remote terminal. A shell account is not a direct connection to the Internet.

signature block A standard block of text at the end of an e-mail message or news article that contains information about the person who originated the message.

SLIP Serial Line Interface Protocol. A data format used to connect a PC to the Internet, using the PC's serial port.

store-and-forward The process of holding messages on a host and transferring them to their ultimate destination.

sub-domain A portion of a DNS address that identifies a smaller group within a larger domain name, such as history.iowa.edu. where history is a sub-domain of the University of Iowa.

subscribe The process of joining a news group in order to receive new articles as they appear.

TCP/IP Transmission Control Protocol/Internet Protocol. The base protocols that are the rules for data format and transmission governing communication over the Internet.

telnet The Internet service protocol that connects one computer to a second computer as a remote terminal.

terminal A device that sends input signals to a computer, usually from a keyboard, and receives output signals from the computer and displays them on a screen or printer.

terminal emulation A computer program that makes the computer's connection to a second computer appear to the second computer as if it was receiving signals from a specific type of terminal. In this way, computers that would otherwise be incompatible can communicate with another.

thread A series of news articles on a single subject, organized with replies immediately following the original message.

Usenet The most formally organized part of the worldwide electronic exchange of news groups. Usenet messages are distributed through the Internet and other electronic information exchange systems.

user name The name that a computer uses to identify a particular user. Used to send and receive mail. In the e-mail address *fredu@qcc.edu*, fredu is the user name.

Uniform Resource Locator (URL) A standard format for identifying the location and name of a file or other resource on the Internet. The World Wide Web uses URLs to identify links.

UUCP Unix to Unix CoPy. A store-and-forward system for exchange of e-mail and news to and from computers that are not directly connected to the Internet.

Veronica Very Easy Rodent Oriented Net-wide Index to Computerized Archives. An Internet service that searches for one or more keywords in Gopher menus.

VT-100 The model number of a computer terminal made by the Digital Equipment Corporation. Since many computers recognize the VT-100's signaling format, it is a standard used by many other terminal makers and terminal emulation programs.

Web browser An application program that downloads World Wide Web pages through the Internet and displays them on a computer.

Web page A document that may be reached through the World Wide Web, and is formatted in Hypertext Markup Language (HTML).

Winsock The Windows Sockets standard that defines the interface between Internet application programs and network connection drivers.

Winsock stack An interface program that converts signals between Winsock-compliant Internet application programs and network drivers.

World Wide Web An Internet service that organizes information into hypertext documents.